ACKNOWLEDGEMENTS

*This publication was made possible, in part, by a generous grant from
The Baird Foundation, as well as by donations from the following individuals:*

Judy and Tom Beecher

Lucy Tretiak Caruso and Ron Caruso

George H. Hyde, Jr.

Mr. and Mrs. Robert J. A. Irwin

Mr. and Mrs. Edward Linder

Norman E. Mack, II

Mr. and Mrs. Robert Lang Miller

Bob and Peggy Moriarty

Edward and Pamela Righter

Karl and Teri Riner

Eric Stenclik and Steve Dietz

Albert B. Wende

Thanks also to the Oakland Place book committee for their gift of time and dedication to this project:
Robert J. A. Irwin, Peggy Moriarty, Albert B. Wende and William J. Williamson, Jr.

First published in the United States of America in 2006
by Buffalo Heritage Unlimited, Buffalo, NY 14222

© 2006 Images Buffalo and Erie County Historical Society and as otherwise noted
© 2006 Landmark Society of the Niagara Frontier | www.landmark-niagara.org
© 2006 Buffalo Heritage Unlimited | www.buffaloheritage.com

BUFFALO
·
HERITAGE
·
UNLIMITED
·

Library of Congress Catalog Card Number: pending
ISBN: 0-9788476-3-6

Book Design by Daniel Wangelin

Printed in the U.S.A.
By Digicon Imaging
Buffalo, NY 14222

Gracious Living in Buffalo
OAKLAND PLACE

Martin Wachadlo

Photography by Charles LaChiusa

A COLLABORATION OF LANDMARK
SOCIETY OF THE NIAGARA FRONTIER &
BUFFALO HERITAGE UNLIMITED, INC

BUFFALO
HERITAGE
UNLIMITED

But to go back to the days when we were young, and Oakland Place was beginning to acquire that air of detached serenity which is its distinguishing mark today.

…this charming backwater of the city, where time seemed to stand still and a group or a score or so of the leading families of the city lived in what was virtually a rustic quietude and peace.

"Oakland Place Cow Out O'Luck 25 Years Ago," *Buffalo Express* (March 14, 1926)

Oakland Place is one of the loveliest residential streets in the city of Buffalo. A hidden treasure best known to its residents, this charming enclave of gracious homes was constructed over a period of eight decades. Oakland Place's impressive homes share an unusually high level of traditional architectural design. This lofty standard testifies to the fact that homeowners in this close-knit community have consistently demanded the best for their neighborhood; many of the homes were designed by Buffalo's most prominent architects. Extending just one block between Summer and Bryant Streets, Oakland Place runs parallel to Elmwood Avenue. Delaware Avenue, which is just to the east, was once the city's grandest residential thoroughfare. Today, Delaware and Elmwood run through the heart of many of Buffalo's most successful and desirable neighborhoods.

The land that comprises the neighborhood was originally part of the vast holdings of the Holland Land Company. Between 1811 and 1813 this company of Dutch investors sold the property that would become Oakland Place to various individuals, including Joseph Ellicott. All complete title searches on the street begin with the name of Dutch investor Wilhem Willink; his fellow investors were collectively identified as "and others." The street did not burst forth immediately. It began to flower around the end of the nineteenth century and soon became one of the loveliest spots in the wondrous architectural garden that is Buffalo.

The City Grows Out

Oakland Place was established during the great expansion of Buffalo in the late nineteenth century. Joseph Ellicott, surveyor and agent of the Holland Land Co. and assistant to Pierre L'Enfant in laying out Washington, D.C., laid out Buffalo in 1804. As the western terminus of the Erie Canal, the village of Buffalo began to prosper following the canal's 1825 opening. Seven years later, the expanding community became the City of Buffalo. Soon thereafter, the metropolis became a principal rail center as well. During the Civil War, the traditional path for shipping Midwestern grain was changed from going down the Mississippi, to

a new route traveling through Buffalo. This shift secured the city's future as a center of commerce and led to a tremendous increase in manufacturing. By the early twentieth century, Buffalo was the eighth-largest city in the United States.

The city's population swelled and new residential areas were developed to meet the demand. For many years, North Street had been the northern border of the city. Although few people lived further north, Buffalo annexed the village of Black Rock in 1853 to provide land for future expansion. Black Rock covered a large geographic area, including the entire upper West Side above North Street. Much of the land was unsettled except for the western section along the waterfront. Delaware Street, one of Buffalo's principal radial boulevards, was an exception. By the 1850s, this thoroughfare was becoming the address of choice for many of Buffalo's leading citizens; in fact, some homes had already been built on the newly annexed section beyond North Street. Soon after the Civil War, this section of the street began to fill with opulent mansions. The prestigious street's name was subsequently changed to Delaware Avenue.

The Birth of Oakland Place

On the west side of Delaware Avenue between Bryant and Summer Streets (which had been laid out by the 1850s), the new homes occupied lots that initially extended all the way west to Rogers Street, which is now Richmond Avenue. Some of the lots—such as those of Isaac and Henry Bryant, which extended along their namesake street from Delaware to Elmwood Avenues—contained orchards and produce gardens in addition to expansive lawns. The rear sections of other lots were used as pasture land for grazing livestock. However, the best return on investment for these long parcels was to sell pieces of them for building lots. The addition of north-south streets was necessary to make this possible.

By 1866, it was determined that three avenues would be placed parallel with Rogers Street: Ashland, Oakland, and Elmwood. All three were to extend north from Summer Street to Ferry Street and beyond. Parts of Elmwood Avenue had already been opened, and the street was progressively lengthened to the north and south over several decades. Elmwood, which had originally been named Oakland, was finally extended into downtown in the early twentieth century. The extension was accomplished by making existing shorter streets part of Elmwood, which accounts for the avenue's meandering path today. Although one avenue had originally been proposed for the area west of Elmwood Avenue, two were in place by the 1880s: Ashland and Howard (now Norwood). Oakland Avenue was to begin just a short

View down tranquil Oakland Place from the
corner of Summer Street, circa 1900.

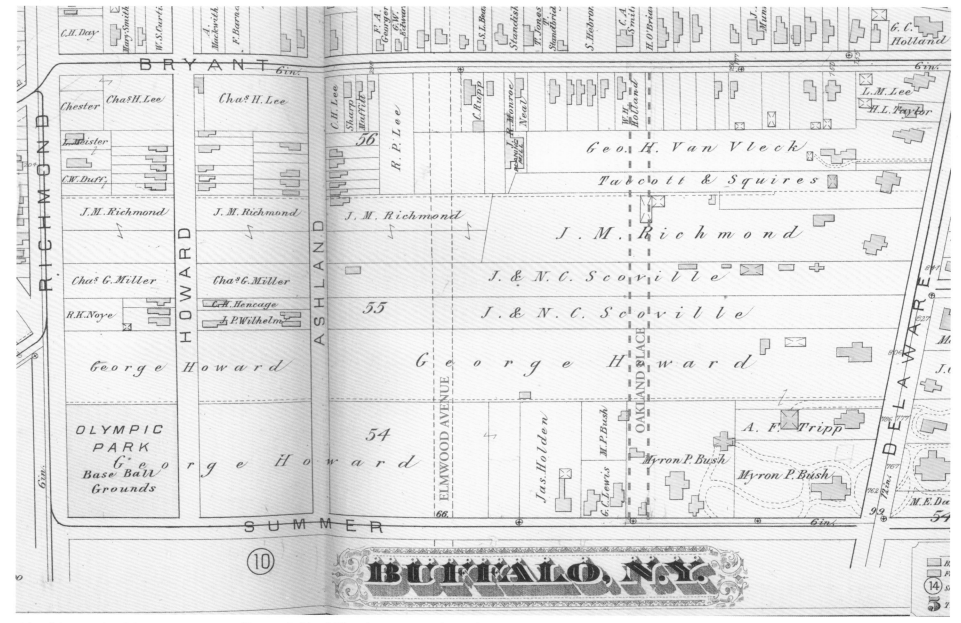

Atlas of the City of Buffalo, New York (1884)　(**Future Oakland Place location noted in red.**)

distance west of Delaware Avenue, but when the street was finally laid out, its position was moved further west to take less property from the Delaware Avenue lots.

In June 1887, a petition for the opening of a new street extending from Summer to Bryant Streets, signed by a majority of affected property owners, was filed before the Buffalo Common Council. Although the proposal was approved, it was rescinded at the end of the year. The reasons for the rescinding were obviously addressed, because the proposal was subsequently reapproved on March 5, 1888. The Common Council's approval included orders that the street be opened, that it be known as Oakland Place, and that the owners of real estate benefited by the opening be assessed $56,166.84 for expenses incurred. Additional assessments were levied for the laying of water, sewer, and gas pipes, placing gaslight street lamps, removing obstructions, and cleaning and filling privy vaults. Four houses stood in the way of the new thoroughfare: 177 Summer Street and 214, 218, and 222 Bryant Street. After being sold at prices ranging from $330 to $3,125, these homes were moved to different locations in the city.

The property owners of Oakland Place also agreed to be assessed $17,678.61 so that the street could be paved with "A. L. Barber's Genuine Trinidad Asphalt Pavement" in 1888. By 1896, half of the asphalt streets in the nation had been paved by this local firm, and Buffalo at that time had more asphalt-paved streets than any city in America. The firm, which was headed by Amzi L. Barber, had briefly included Barber's brother-in-law, John J. Albright, one of the city's most prominent millionaire industrialists. Albright was also a major philanthropist; one of his legacies to Buffalo is the art gallery that bears his name. Albright later invested heavily in Barber's Locomobile Company, but when the firm failed around World War I, it took Albright's vast fortune with it. Though Albright did not live on Oakland Place, two of his children did. A daughter, Ruth, lived at 115, while a son, Langdon, lived in two Oakland Place homes, 33 and 120.

In May of 1893, a proposal to extend Oakland Place to Clinton (now Potomac) Avenue was placed before the Buffalo Common Council. The Council tabled the item and Oakland Place remained one block long.

This circa 1892 view looking northwest from the tower of Westminster Presbyterian Church shows Summer Street (extending from lower right to upper left) and the southern end of Oakland Place (extending to the right). *Columbian Year Book: Buffalo and Niagara Falls, N.Y.* (1893)   BUFFALO & ERIE COUNTY HISTORICAL SOCIETY

Oakland Place was originally the home of upper middle class Buffalonians. Although it may have seemed logical for the elite families of Delaware Avenue to create family compounds by building homes for their siblings or children on Oakland Place, there are only two such cases: the Goodyears (123) and the Knoxes (57). Three sons of Stephen M. Clement, Jr., eventually lived in preexisting homes (29/33) behind their mother's Delaware Avenue home. The street did become popular with the children of Buffalo's wealthiest citizens. It boasted such prominent names as Albright (33, 115, 120), Schoellkopf (48), and Sidway (22, 37, 38). Life on Oakland Place was often a family affair: having at least one relative or in-law as an Oakland Place neighbor was a frequent occurrence. In fact, the lure of Oakland Place was (and is) so strong that it was not uncommon for residents to part with one home in favor of another down the block.

The practice of law was, by far, the most popular profession for Oakland Place residents. The street could have been nicknamed "Attorney's Alley" because so many of Buffalo's best legal minds called the street home. Lyman M. Bass, James McCormick Mitchell, Norris Morey, Robert W. Pomeroy, and Henry Ware Sprague were among the notable resident lawyers. Industrialists, merchants, and clergymen were also well represented. In fact, Oakland Place was the location of the Trinity Episcopal Church rectory for five decades. The street was also home to partners in three of Buffalo's largest department stores: James N. Adam (60) of J. N. Adam & Co.; William Anderson (80) of Adam, Meldrum & Anderson (AM&As); and Herbert A. Meldrum (88) of H. A. Meldrum & Co. Adam's career was not limited to his department store; it also included public service. While living on Oakland Place he was a three-term mayor of Buffalo.

The ladies of Oakland Place played a significant role in the development of the street. Women were often clients, commissioning complete original designs as well as alterations to many homes. They were also property owners. Property rights were then one of the few areas in which women and men had complete equality. Women had a great influence on the design of their houses, as the home was widely considered the proper place for a "lady" to spend most of her time. Thus the appearance of Oakland Place was largely shaped by the tastes of the daughters, wives, and widows of the men who are usually given credit for creating the city.

The Development of Oakland Place

Fences, walls and hedges toward the street are abolished, and the long vistas of Delaware, Linwood and Richmond avenues, Chapin, Bidwell and Lincoln parkways, Bryant, North, West Ferry, Summer, and many other fine residence streets are unmarred by barriers, one lawn melting imperceptibly into the next, the exact boundaries of the several estates being known only in the city surveyor's office. This absence of fences produces a very pleasing effect, possibly in some cases illusory, of neighborly kindness and fellowship. At all events, vision and light and breezes have a liberal sweep down the long green colonnades; nor are fingers or feet often tempted beyond resistance by the gorgeous flowers and velvet turf so freely displayed.
"Home Life in Buffalo," *Good Housekeeping* (Aug. 1901)

Oakland Place could–and should–have been added to the above list of the "fine residence streets" of Buffalo. This paragraph perfectly sums up the impression of people, both past and present, who visit the city and appreciate one of its chief glories: an abundance of fine freestanding homes on individual lots. So it was that Oakland Place developed in the years before World War I. Some of the lots were less than 50 feet wide, as was typical of many middle and upper-middle class streets. Others, at well over 100 feet wide, were more in line with the grand estates of Delaware Avenue. A wide variety of homes, with a range of architectural styles and designs, were built on these lots. The cohesiveness of the ensemble was due in large part to the long vistas of green lawns and the "long green colonnades" of Elm trees that once arched over the streetscape.

Though some Oakland Place homes occupy spacious lots, others, as in many areas of the city, are situated quite close to neighboring homes. Many people in the modern age wonder why large homes were constructed on relatively narrow lots, especially in cases where there is not even enough room for a driveway. When Oakland Place was young, street frontage for a lot in a desirable neighborhood was quite expensive; the cost of labor and materials for building a house was comparatively less so. Thus, it was the width of the lot rather than the size of the home that was the true outward sign of wealth. But what of the need for a driveway leading back to the stable? The reality was that it was (and is) very costly to own a horse: the animal had to be housed, fed, groomed, and exercised

The grand Shingle style house at 173 Summer Street (circa 1887) was designed by Green & Wicks. Edward B. Green would later live across the street at 178 Summer Street, with a fine view onto rapidly developing Oakland Place, but his firm is known to have designed only one house on that street (77).

daily, and this involved additional staff. Only the very wealthy, and those who owned vehicles as part of their businesses, could afford to keep horses on their properties. Others boarded their horses and stored their carriages at the livery stables around the city, but most people, even many who were well off, walked or rode the streetcars. Most homes in the city were built for the requirements of the time. The idea that most people would own automobiles, and want to park them near their homes, is a fairly modern one; it is not something that the original owners of Oakland Place's grand homes had to consider.

Interestingly, the oldest houses on Oakland Place actually predate the construction of the street, and some of the houses originally stood elsewhere. The home at 138 has the distinction of being the oldest: it was built circa 1874 as a simple front-gable Italianate home at 226 Bryant Street. In the late 1920s, it was substantially enlarged and reoriented towards Oakland Place; thus, it was changed to an Oakland Place address without ever moving from its original location. This is not true of the second oldest house on the street, 22. This home was evidently built in the Second Empire style, circa 1876, and stood at 201 Summer Street. In 1890, it was moved to its present location so that a new

Childrens Hospital

Elmwood School

First Congregational Church

56

1386 to West Line

1310.75 to W Line Lot

1310.25 to West Line

55

54

ASHLAND

ELMWOOD AVENUE

OAKLAND

DELAWARE AVENUE

New Century Atlas of Greater Buffalo (1915)
CANISIUS COLLEGE

SUMMER STREET

9

This Queen Anne style home, which no longer stands, was built for William Anderson at 80 Oakland Place in 1893. Circa 1901 view.

Moving old buildings was quite common in the nineteenth and early twentieth centuries. Some buildings were moved a mile or two to new sites and many were moved much shorter distances. In this way, the effort, cost, and natural resources expended to build the house it were not discarded. Even when buildings were taken down, they were actually dismantled piece by piece and most of the materials were cleaned and sold for reuse. This is in stark contrast to the dumping of entire buildings into landfills that is the rule today.

The large houses that stand at the corners of Summer Street, like twin sentinels at the foot of Oakland Place, also predate the establishment of Oakland. A large Shingle-style house, 173 Summer Street was built circa 1887 for banker Stephen M. Clement, Jr., (1859-1913) and his family. They lived in the house until the early 1890s. The Clements later built the grand Tudor mansion at 786 Delaware Avenue, which today houses the local headquarters of the American Red Cross. Three of Clement's sons, Norman, Harold, and Stewart, later lived on Oakland Place, at 29, 33, and 116. Later, 173 Summer Street was occupied by William Henry Hotchkiss (not to be confused with William Horace Hotchkiss of 37) and his wife. It was said that though the Hotchkiss home "really faced on Summer, [they] always counted as Oaklandites." The second sentinel, a Stick-style house at 185 Summer Street, was designed in 1883 for George Sweet, whose company manufactured baby carriages. This home acquired the address of 2 Oakland Place when it was converted to apartments after World War II.

mansion could be constructed on its old site. Grocer Frederick C. Williams was the first occupant at 22. Later, Charles B. Hill, a lawyer and the center of an Oakland Place mystery, lived there. (see page 29)

The houses at 123 and 135 were both built on Bryant Street, and were moved to Oakland Place in the early twentieth century to make way for new construction. Timber tycoon Charles W. Goodyear and his wife, Ella Conger, completed their enormous French Renaissance mansion at 888 Delaware Avenue in 1903. Their home had extensive grounds that extended back to Oakland Place. Two of their children subsequently built mansions along Bryant Street. One house that stood in the way of construction was moved to 123 Oakland Place, where it became a home for a third Goodyear child in 1912, Charles W. Goodyear, Jr., and his family. In 1911, industrialist William W. Smith and his wife, Mary, sold their Bryant Street property to Children's Hospital for the construction of a new nurses' home, designed by Lansing, Bley & Lyman. But the Smiths decided to keep their circa 1887 Queen Anne style home and had it moved to 135 Oakland Place.

The first new house on the street was built circa 1888 by industrialist William D. Olmsted on a large lot that backed up to the Delaware Avenue estate of Olmsted's in-law, George B. Matthews. This large Queen Anne style house featured a stone first story, frame above, and a profusion of porches and gables. The style, characterized by a picturesque silhouette, varied surfaces, and rich detailing, was derived from late medieval English architecture and had little to do with the reign of Queen Anne. Introduced to America in 1874 by architect H. H. Richardson, the Queen Anne style soon became extremely popular. In fact, it was the style of choice for residential architecture in Buffalo near the end of the nineteenth century. There were other Queen Anne homes on Oakland Place: 80 was designed for department store proprietor William Anderson, of Adam, Meldrum & Anderson, and 88 was designed for dredging contractor Edward J. Hingston. The houses now located at 123 and 135 were also designed in the Queen Anne style.

The Shingle style grew out of the Queen Anne style. In this new style, volume and massing were the dominant elements; the exterior was unified with the use of wood shingles over most or all of the surfaces, including the roof. Originally called Old Colonial, it was inspired by the shingled vernacular buildings of seventeenth-century America. The finest example of the Shingle style on Oakland Place is the home at 32, designed in 1890 for Clarissa F. Griffin, who unfortunately did not live to see it completed. The imposing Edward Roth house at 102 features a Richardsonian Romanesque brick base with a beautifully detailed shingled superstructure above, while the Bright Taber house next door at 100 and William H. Boughton's Rev. Henry Adams house across the street at 103 incorporate Colonial Revival elements into a Shingle style composition.

Oakland Place featured fine examples of residential designs that did not fit neatly into one stylistic category. A gifted architect had the ability to mix architectural styles with aplomb; Buffalo was very fortunate in having a number of such designers. The massive homes that architect C. D. Swan designed for Louis Schoellkopf at 48 and James Horton at 60 were essentially Shingle-style homes rendered in brick and stone and were comparable in impression to the grand houses designed by H. H. Richardson. A similar Richardsonian feel is present in the large residence at 120, designed in 1895 by Martin C. Miller for Anna F. Walbridge, wife of hardware store magnate and Civil War veteran Charles F. Walbridge.

The popularity of the Shingle style was accompanied by an increasing interest in the nation's colonial past as a design source. Architects eventually shifted their focus from the vernacular to the more formal prototypes of the eighteenth and early nineteenth centuries, resulting in a new style known as Colonial Revival. Examples executed in brick are often called Georgian Revival. The hallmarks of the style are symmetry, formality, and classical detailing. The Colonial Revival style had the added benefit of strong allusions to the early history of the nation. Nearly all of Buffalo's old families had roots in colonial New England, and using this style allowed homeowners to celebrate this heritage in their homes. The Margaret Shortiss house, constructed in 1890 at 64 Oakland Place, was one of the earliest examples of the style in Buffalo, and was the first of many on the street. Colonial Revival became the dominant architectural style on Oakland Place. Several homes show the range of expression possible with the style: Boughton & Johnson's Robert W. Pomeroy residence at 70, designed in 1896, is a study in elegance; the Hotchkiss house at 37, designed in 1897 by Lansing & Beierl, shows the exuberant side of the style; and Wood & Bradney's 1916 design of George A. Jackson's home at 87 is a more restrained version. It is a testament to the enduring nature of the style that Colonial Revival homes continued to be erected on Oakland Place until the latter part of the twentieth century.

The asymmetrical medieval tradition was an alternative to the symmetrical, classically detailed Colonial Revival style. The disparate elements of the medieval tradition fall within the category of Tudor or Tudor Revival (regardless of whether those elements had their origin during the reign of the Tudors); other terms, including Elizabethan, Jacobean, or Tudorbethan, have also been used to describe this style. Lansing & Beierl's 28 Oakland Place, designed in 1901 for linseed oil manufacturer John A. Mann, was the first example of the Tudor style on the street. The interior, however, is Colonial Revival. Perhaps the medieval exterior and colonial interior were the result of a compromise between a husband and wife with different tastes. Wood & Bradney's Wilson residence at 95, designed in 1913, shows the freedom of design possible with the style in the hands of talented architects. However, the Tudor style really did not come into its own on Oakland Place until the 1920s.

The Craftsman style, a development of the medieval tradition, avoided overt references to the past in favor of an original and simple form of expression. The best example of the Craftsman style on Oakland Place is 143. It was designed in 1914 by Stephen R. Berry and is unique on the street because it was built as a double house by a developer, rather than as a single-family home for an individual. Lansing & Beierl's 129 Oakland Place was designed in 1907 for the reform-minded lawyer Lyman Bass. The exterior provides a well-rendered example of the style; the interior, in a bow to tradition, is Colonial Revival. The Craftsman style was more popular with progressive middle-class businessmen and speculative builders than with the conservative upper classes of the city, who preferred buildings with a more identifiable historic pedigree. One successful businessman open to building a progressive Craftsman home was Darwin D. Martin, but his architect declined the opportunity to design a home on Oakland Place.

Frank Lloyd Wright and Oakland Place

Early in the twentieth century Frank Lloyd Wright designed a home for Darwin D. Martin, the wealthy secretary of the Larkin Soap Company. This home, in Buffalo's Parkside neighborhood, has since become an iconic example of Wright's architecture. However, Martin's original intention was for Wright to design the house for a lot on Oakland Place. In 1901, Darwin and his wife, Isabelle, decided to move out of their first house in the middle-class Parkside neighborhood, wanting to live among people of their new social status. Darwin

The dining room of 33 Oakland Place, arranged for an elegant dinner party.

12

Martin was reputedly the highest-paid business executive in the country, and as a result, the Martins had their choice of any neighborhood in the city of Buffalo. For Darwin and Isabelle, Oakland Place was the logical choice. In December, they purchased the lot that would become 110. They paid $15,000 for the property—a testament to the land values of Oakland Place.

Before his plans to build had taken definite shape, Darwin toured the Chicago suburb of Oak Park with his brother, William, in September 1902. The brothers were impressed by the houses of Frank Lloyd Wright, but Wright was out of the office during their visit. The following month, William, who lived in Chicago, met the architect. William immediately wrote to Darwin; calling Wright "one of nature's noblemen," he implored Darwin to hire Wright as architect for his new house. However, when told of Darwin's Oakland Place lot, Frank Lloyd Wright said "it would be a pity" to build his design on a lot only 75 feet wide, unless the adjacent houses were set back considerably to allow for a sweeping view of the new house. At the end of October, Darwin wrote to William, indicating his intention to stick with Oakland Place:

> On both sides of my 75' lot the houses stand very near my line, but the house line is about 75' from the sidewalk. This provides sweep enough to give a view of both sides of my house. Anyhow, $15,000 worth of land is all I can afford.

Darwin Martin's desire to build on Oakland Place was no match for Frank Lloyd Wright's legendary powers of persuasion. Wright visited Buffalo in November, saw the Martins' Oakland Place lot, and was not pleased. The architect convinced Darwin that what he really wanted was a large corner lot in the Parkside neighborhood, just down the street from where he was already living:

> The lot Mr. Wright likes is the northwest corner of Jewett and Summit Aves. Diagonally opposite the church. There is 207' on Jewett Ave. and 261' on Summit. The west line of the lot parallel to Summit is 317' deep. The plot contains 1¼ acres. The assessed valuation is $10,300. I have tried all summer to buy it for $12,000. The owners want $17,000. I have finally told the owner's representative that if he would submit to me an option on the place for $14,000 I would consider it. I expect it will be quite a stunt to sell the Oakland Place lot and it costs nearly $1,000 per year to carry it. I won't let Wright build so expensive [a] house as you suggest.
> (Darwin Martin to William Martin, December 10, 1902. The letters quoted here are held in the Archives of the State University of New York at Buffalo.)

Like his desire to live on Oakland Place, Martin's intention to not let Wright build an expensive house was thwarted by the inimitable architect.

The fact that the mid-block Oakland Place lot was worth about the same as the much larger Parkside corner lot is indicative of the prestige of the street. Still, Darwin found that "buyers are mighty scarce." Whether it was due to lack of buyers or a price that was too steep, the Martins did not immediately sell their Oakland Place lot. Despite the fact that it cost "nearly $1,000 per year to carry it," they held it even after their new Jewett Parkway home was completed. In an effort to get some return on the investment, Martin asked Wright to design an apartment building for the site in late 1908, which would have been the first such building on the street. One can only imagine what the conservative residents of Oakland Place would have thought of having one of Wright's avant garde designs in their midst. These plans never came to fruition, but the following year an apartment house of traditional styling was built directly across the street, at 107. The Martins finally sold the property at 110 Oakland Place in early 1909, and a Colonial Revival house was immediately erected there.

The Porch Culture

Despite differences in styles, expansive front porches or verandas were important features of the earliest homes built on Oakland Place:

> Those were the days of veranda life, when the lady of the house, having seen to everything indoors, emerged in mid morning and took up her position in one of the porch rockers, armed with sewing or reading. Bright nods and greetings were exchanged with neighboring verandas, the time of the day was passed with the postman, the itinerant fishman, the grocer's boy and stray dogs and cats and babies who happened along, and the long, golden days slipped by into evening before they had scarce begun. Sometimes there were little veranda parties, of the thimble and tea type, and when the men came home at night, the smoke of their post-prandial cigars and the rustle of the last editions marked the end of a perfect day.
> "Oakland Place Cow Out O'Luck 25 Years Ago," *Buffalo Express* (March 14, 1926)

The porch culture so glowingly described here was already a distant memory when the article was written in 1926. The porches had a significant practical drawback: they drastically reduced the amount of light entering the first floor. This was an important concern in the days before powerful artificial light. With the advent of the automobile and changes in lifestyle, the focus shifted away from the street and into the back yard, where a rear terrace with a retractable awning became the preferred outdoor space. As new homes were constructed on the street in the early years of the twentieth century, front porches became progressively smaller, and they disappeared entirely in the new homes built after World War I. In the 1920s, people began removing existing porches as they remodeled and updated their homes. However, the front porch is making a comeback, and in recent years the porches and verandas of yesterday have begun to reappear on some Oakland Place homes (119 and 123).

Inside Oakland Place

The keen and gusty winters are made to many hearts the most precious season of the year by the indrawing of friends and comrades, and the increased social activity in a hundred overlapping circles, from the sumptuous private and public balls and elaborate dinners and banquets, to modest coteries of readers and card players. "Home Life in Buffalo," *Good Housekeeping* (Aug. 1901)

The grand house was more than just a place for the family to live; it was also emblematic of the owner's social status. While the home's exterior symbols of status were displayed to the world at large, the interior symbols were reserved for one's peers. The first floor was the public space of the house and it was the setting for the social rituals that were so much a part of life during the period. In the tile-floored vestibule, wet or snow-caked outer garments and boots were removed, often with the assistance of a servant. One then entered a large main hall with a grand staircase rising to the family's private space on the second floor. All of the principal rooms of the first floor were accessed through wide openings off the main hall. Pocket doors or curtains were closed when intimate spaces were required and left open when a large space was needed for an event. Each home had a living room or library and a dining room. The larger ones often had additional rooms, including a parlor, sitting room, den, loggia, or conservatory. The principal rooms often had fireplaces, which served as amenities rather than necessities, because all of the homes on Oakland Place had central heating. Beyond the dining room, a pantry provided access to the kitchen. The pantry served as a place to put finishing touches on food, and also insolated the dining room from the noise of a busy kitchen. Upstairs, the bedrooms were located off the hall at the top of the main staircase. Every residence on Oakland Place had at least one bathroom and many homes had more than one.

Although the homes on Oakland Place were known for their distinguished occupants, most housed servants as well. Each Oakland Place home had two staircases, one in the front and one in the rear. Servants used the rear staircase to move throughout the house without disturbing the resident family. Cooking, cleaning, and general maintenance were onerous tasks that required a great deal of time and effort, especially because labor-saving devices such as vacuum cleaners and washing machines were just coming into general usage. As a result, occupants of the homes, if they could afford to, employed staff. Many families, even among Buffalo's middle class, had a maid, and the more affluent families had several.

Members of the household staff were an important element of life in these grand homes. Nearly every house on Oakland Place had at least one live-in servant in the years before World War II. There was even a live-in servant in each apartment at 107 Oakland Place. The larger homes had larger staffs; 70, for example, had five live-in servants as late as 1930. These servants were almost always single women. Sometimes a male chauffeur and his family lived in the carriage house, but most male staff lived elsewhere. Additional help was hired for parties and other major events. In most of the homes on Oakland Place, the third-floor servant's quarters are intact; some even have the original bathrooms. These time capsules survived by accident in many cases. After the servants departed, the third floor often became storage space and never required updating.

The servants were kept busy with the day-to-day tasks inherent to a large residence, but they were especially taxed during the large parties that were a regular part of life in a grand home. Mabel Dodge Luhan, nee Ganson, who grew up nearby at 675 Delaware Avenue, offered a vivid description of a turn-of-the-century dinner party in her 1933 memoir, *Intimate Memories*:

There stood the long table covered with flashing glass and silver, every kind of wine and water glass, three or four of them at each place, and four or five knives and forks. Dozens of small silver dishes filled with candy and sweetmeats covered the lace center-piece, and in the middle of the table a huge silver bowl was filled to overflowing with pink roses. Oh, the sight and smell of a dinner party! How my heart contracts as I write of my first one!

The loaded table stood in the subdued light of the room, glistening and portentous, like a sumptuous altar before the god descends upon it. I heard the maids in the pantry conversing in the low, serious voices that the occasion produced in them. Such a party was always a severe ordeal for them all in the kitchen. Twelve guests and nearly twelve courses of food, dozens and dozens of delicate glasses to be cared for, dozens and dozens of costly china places; and all these dishes to be served promptly without a break in the rhythm – one thing followed another smoothly, inevitably. The wine bottles standing in rows ready to be uncorked, for every glass must always be full; the accessories ready waiting at the side; the crackers and cheeses and jellies and sauces, the pickles and sauces and olives and relishes.

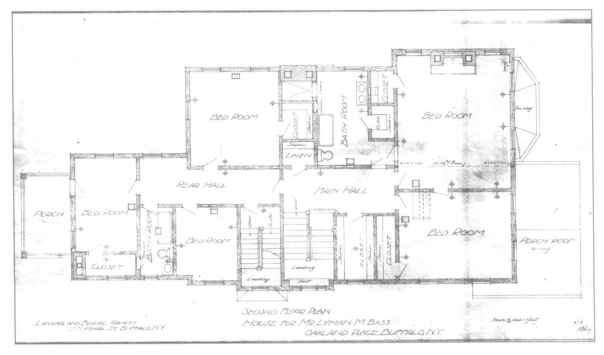

SECOND FLOOR PLAN
HOUSE FOR MR. LYMAN M. BASS
OAKLAND PLACE, BUFFALO, N.Y.

FRONT ELEVATION

WALL SECTION
RESIDENCE FOR MR. LYMAN M. BASS
OAKLAND PL. BUFFALO. N.Y.

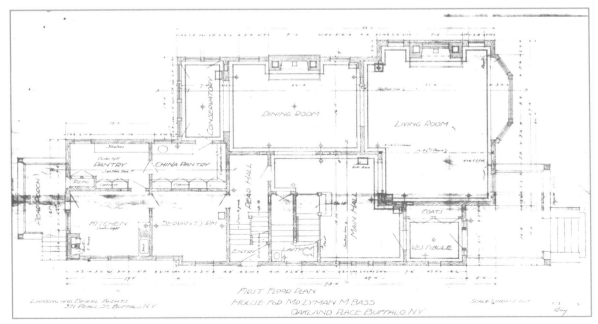

FIRST FLOOR PLAN
HOUSE FOR MR. LYMAN M. BASS
OAKLAND PLACE, BUFFALO, N.Y.

The house of Lyman M. Bass at 129 Oakland Place (see pages 110-111) was designed by Lansing & Beierl in 1907. The architect's original plans provide a good representation of residential design during the period.

Above: The front elevation also shows the house in section. Drawn by draftsman Albert J. Schallmo. The house assumed its present appearance when it was expanded to the north in 1911; the addition was by successor firm Lansing, Bley & Lyman.

Left: First and second floor plans. Drawn by draftsman (and future partner) Lawrence H. Bley (rhymes with eye). The porch is only half the width of the façade, and thus does not cut off light from the living room. Note the open floor plan and the proximity of the main staircase and adjacent back stairs.

DAVID & BARRIE KOEHLER

The substantial Main Building of Children's Hospital (1906-1908), at 219 Bryant Street, was designed by Green & Wicks. Though this building was demolished around 1969, the adjacent Nurses' Home (1911), designed by Lansing, Bley & Lyman, still stands. Circa 1930 view.

In the Neighborhood

Soon after the street was opened, some notable Buffalo institutions were established in the vicinity, making Oakland Place an even more desirable place to live. Perhaps the most significant new institutional neighbor was Children's Hospital. This facility has continued to be a dominant presence at the head of Oakland Place to this day. Dr. Bainbridge Folwell, a prominent local physician, believed that children should not be cared for in adult hospital wards, where they could see and hear the seriously ill and dying. Persuaded by Folwell's ideas, Mrs. Gibson T. Williams and her daughter Martha purchased a brick house at 219 Bryant Street for a twelve-bed hospital, which opened in September 1892. (Mrs. Williams' sons lived in the grand McKim, Mead & White-designed mansions at 672 and 690 Delaware Avenue.) The hospital subsequently expanded into adjacent houses along Bryant and Hodge Streets, and in 1908, a new two-story hospital building was opened. The new structure had an excellent view of Oakland Place.

The Elmwood School was also an important institution at the head of Oakland Place. This exclusive private school was founded as a kindergarten on West Utica Street in 1889. The school moved to a newly constructed brick building at 213 Bryant Street, adjacent to the new Children's Hospital, in October 1892. The Elmwood School was described as an oasis in an educational desert, offering a progressive, coeducational program for children in kindergarten and grades one through eight. There was a high school for a time, as well. Pupils of the Elmwood School came from Buffalo's best families: Bryant Street was thick with the carriages of the wealthy as they (or their servants) took the children to school in the morning and picked them up at the end of the school day. The pupils appreciated the school's location. The large, open lot at the southeast corner of Bryant Street and Oakland Place was "their favorite foregathering place, which was lush with fruit trees and had a rolling, grassy terrain ideal for any kind of game during recess, on Saturdays or when playing hookey."

Perhaps it was appropriate that these institutions dedicated to the young were located here, for the Oakland Place neighborhood was described thus:

Elmwood School, 213 Bryant Street, circa 1930.
ELMWOOD FRANKLIN SCHOOL

[It] was fairly overrun with children, rosy cheeked, wholesome and active boys and girls who proved the oft-disputed statement that children really love to play in the street better than anywhere else. For they used to come from their own yards and gardens, from surrounding streets and even distant sections of the city, to play on the pavement of Oakland place all day long, winter and summer. The hop scotch marks on the asphalt remained bright and unblurred day after day, for the traffic was practically nil, and prisoner's base, to say nothing of pom-pom-pullaway, beckon, every man his own goal, hide and seek in the orchard lots, and plain tag, all claimed the passionate and undivided attention of a full aristocratic youngsters [sic] in this particular spot which was as safely guarded against public encroachment as if it had had the gateways at each end for which Miss Beecher [32] tried long but unsuccessfully.

"Oakland Place Cow Out O'Luck 25 Years Ago," *Buffalo Express* (March 14, 1926)

Oakland Place was ideal for their affluent parents, as well. Its location provided convenient access to downtown; some residents walked or rode bicycles to work and made use of the streetcar in inclement weather. Others, of course, traveled in chauffeur-driven carriages or cars; some of these vehicles were garaged elsewhere and summoned to Oakland Place as needed.

Private clubs were a quintessential element in the lives of Buffalo's elite, and several of these clubs were located in convenient proximity to Oakland Place. The Garret Club was founded in 1902 by young women from leading families for the sole purpose of having fun. In 1903, the women moved their club into an older home (no longer in existence) at 205 Bryant Street, near the head of Oakland Place. The diminutive dwelling was known as the "toy clubhouse." The new club soon became very popular; in fact, membership soon expanded to include older women who were "girls in spirit." Many of the women living on Oakland Place were members, not having to travel far to enjoy their club. In 1916, though, the club moved to its present location on Cleveland Avenue. Just as that club left the immediate vicinity of Oakland Place, another one opened around the corner. The Buffalo Tennis Club, at 314 Elmwood Avenue, provided a perfect venue for one of the most popular physical activities of the day. The newly constructed building, designed in 1915 by Lansing, Bley & Lyman, featured both tennis and squash courts, and the club was later renamed the Buffalo Tennis and Squash Club.

The residents of Oakland Place were further heartened when one of the city's most exclusive organizations, the Saturn Club, moved to 977 Delaware Avenue from its previous home at Delaware Avenue and Edward Street. The club's new home, a grand Tudor-style building designed by Bley & Lyman, was opened in

Some of the earliest members of the Garret Club are shown enjoying themselves on the front porch of the "Toy Clubhouse" at 205 Bryant Street circa 1905.

GARRET CLUB

1922. (The building that had previously housed the Saturn Club was sold to the Montefiore Club, which occupied the building until it was destroyed by fire in 1969. The Montefiore Club then moved to the Knox mansion at 800 Delaware Avenue.) Socially, the Saturn Club was one of the most important clubs in the city. Almost all male residents of Oakland Place were members, and many of them served as its dean. (This club's officials have collegiate titles, such as dean, registrar, and bursar.) Like many social institutions of the time, the Saturn Club admitted men only, which was reflected in the club's motto: "Where the Women Cease from Troubling and the Wicked are at Rest" (recently revised). However, in a section of the club accessible via a side door, women could dine with their husbands. This dining room was especially popular on Thursdays, because maids generally had that night off. The city's elite made do in the absence of household staff by dining in private clubs. The Saturn Club, which began admitting women in 1989, still counts many Oakland Place residents among its membership.

The Changing Neighborhood:
The Roaring Twenties & the Great Depression

With the construction of the Jackson house at 87 Oakland Place in 1916, nearly all of the lots on the street were filled, but the lure of the neighorhood remained very strong during the boom years of the 1920s—so strong, in fact, that the lack of vacant lots did not deter the construction of the grandest mansions on the street. In 1924 Mrs. Seymour H. Knox, Sr., of 800 Delaware Avenue, commissioned a grand Georgian Revival home for her son Seymour, Jr., to be built on the vacant lot (57) at the rear of her property. She also intended to build an adjacent home for one of her daughters, and so demolished 61, which had stood for just over twenty years. Unfortunately this second home was never built and that lot has remained a sunken garden. (The stable behind 61 became the garage of 57.) As the residence of one of Buffalo's wealthiest citizens, 57 was one of the showplaces of the city and the scene of many lavish and exclusive parties.

In 1927, Mrs. Georgia M. G. Forman purchased 79 Oakland Place, the first house to be built on the street. Mrs. Forman, who had been married to an oil millionaire, immediately demolished the house and commissioned the leading architectural firm of "Edward B. Green & Sons—Albert Hart Hopkins" to design one of the grandest Tudor Revival homes in the city. This new home became 77 Oakland Place, and is the only home on the street that Green's firm is known to have designed. The division of the backyard at 226 Bryant Street also provided opportunities for building and expanding. In 1919, construction magnate John W. Cowper of 124 Oakland Place added to his property by purchasing a portion of this divided backyard. In 1928, he took advantage of the expanded space by demolishing his existing home and building a grand Tudor manse in its place. The new home, designed by Hudson & Hudson, bore the address of 126 Oakland Place. Mrs. Anna Burnett also appreciated the opportunity that dividing the Bryant Street backyard provided: in 1921 she had a Colonial Revival house built on her tiny lot at 130 Oakland Place.

These new homes on Oakland Place had an effect upon the owners of older homes: they felt the need to keep up with the changing architectural tastes of the 1920s. On the exterior, this usually involved removing the porch and sometimes meant installing a newer model doorway. Sometimes, however, the exterior changes were more drastic: at 119, the entire exterior was covered with stucco to create a Tudor style effect. (This stucco coating was recently removed from the front of the house to reveal the original exterior finish.) In addition, homeowners made significant interior changes. In some rooms, Victorian details were stripped and more modern touches were added, new bathrooms were often installed, and, in some cases, rooms were added to the back of the house. Some of the changes were extreme. Although the house at 110 Oakland Place was less than twenty years old, the interior was gutted in 1928 and completely remodeled according to designs by Frederick C. Backus.

The 1920s brought changes to the neighborhood around Oakland Place as well, and some residents argued that these changes were not for the better. They were dismayed to witness exclusive residential sections of Delaware and Elmwood Avenues evolving into commercial districts. They were scandalized as once grand mansions became rooming houses or were replaced by stores and offices. To forestall such changes and maintain Oakland Place's ambiance and property values, the owners entered into a deed restriction agreement. Dated February 20, 1928, the agreement outlined the intent of the residents: "whereas said owners are desirous that said Oakland Place should be preserved for a term of years strictly as a residential thoroughfare as nearly as possible to its present state…". The following provisions were included in the agreement:

1. That no building shall be erected, placed, used or maintained on the respective premises owned by the parties hereto, or any part thereof, other than a not more than two family private dwelling house for the purpose of a private residence only, except the apartment house now or formerly owned by the estate of Norris Morey, deceased, and other than a private garage, barn and outbuildings which shall not be nearer to said Oakland Place than the rear of such dwelling house.

2. That no goods or merchandise of any kind shall be manufactured or sold on the respective premises owned by the parties hereto and that neither any business or any trade, professional or otherwise (except doctors' offices) shall be carried on said premises and that no residence shall be partially or wholly used or occupied as a clubhouse.

All owners of property that fronted Oakland Place were parties to the agreement; they were also joined by the owners of 173 and 185 Summer Street, at the foot of Oakland Place. John B. Richards, owner of 226 Bryant Street, opted out. Richards had plans to make modifications to his house, realized later in the year, and his newly enlarged house became known as 138 Oakland Place. Though the agreement expired in 1938, it was subsequently extended to 1948 and again to 1958. At some point, the owners of 173 and 185 Summer Street opted out of the agreement: 173 Summer Street became a rooming house in 1943; 185 Summer Street was converted to apartments in 1949 and became 2 Oakland Place.

The Great Depression and World War II had serious effects on the lifestyle of Oakland Place residents. Most had weathered the economic fiasco of the 1930s reasonably well, but, generally, most new construction and major renovations were put off until better times. During the Depression, many of the city's largest and finest mansions were demolished by their owners because they no longer desired to pay for the upkeep or taxes. This trend hit Oakland Place in 1940: two of the older houses, 80 and 88, were leveled, although their respective stables were left standing and converted into residences. Following America's entry into World War II, there was a tremendous need for women to fill the jobs vacated by men going off to military service. For residents of Oakland Place, this usually meant that live-in maids and cooks left to earn more money in factories and offices. Many Oakland Place matrons found themselves working in their own kitchens for the first time, but everyone considered it a small sacrifice for the war effort. After the war, many servants' quarters remained unoccupied. Men drove their own cars and women did the cooking and hired day maids to take care of the chores and provide extra kitchen help for parties. This austerity did not apply to those who still had considerable wealth; the Knox family, for example, continued to employ uniformed servants at 57.

Traditional design on postwar Oakland Place: architect Duane Lyman's own house at 78 (1949-1950) and Gordon Hayes' Gates house at 88 (1954).

The Postwar Years

After World War II, great prosperity fueled a desire among Americans for a new way of life. For many people, this meant moving from crowded cities filled with old buildings to new, wide-open tract developments outside city limits. They aspired to drive in shiny new automobiles rather than ride on streetcars or buses. Although this trend eventually had adverse effects on most neighborhoods in Buffalo, Oakland Place was unscathed. The serene street retained its charm and continued to be among the most desirable places to live in Western New York. Duane Lyman, a prominent architect, was among the first to leave Buffalo behind in favor of suburban life. However, after more than four decades in the suburbs, he returned to live in the city, chosing Oakland Place, where his first partner, Williams Lansing, had once lived at 29. Lyman designed a small Georgian Revival home in 1949 and lived in the house for the remainder of his days. The house, at

78 Oakland Place, occupies the site where 80 was located prior to its demolition.

Many Buffalo neighborhoods suffered architectural degradation during this time, but Oakland Place did not. The high standards of traditional architectural design that had characterized this Buffalo block since its inception were maintained. The banal, functionalist new buildings and incongruous, cheaply constructed renovations that appeared throughout the city were kept at bay in this little enclave. Developer Hubert (Hugh) Perry guided the development of Oakland Place during the second half of the twentieth century. Perry was known for his skill at elegantly adapting traditional design for modern needs. For both Perry and the residents of Oakland Place, the Colonial past remained an appropriate architectural expression for contemporary life. Although Duane Lyman, Buffalo's leading architect of the period, lived on Oakland Place, he did not play a role in translating Perry's visions into reality. Both men had strong personalities and they evidently disliked each other. Perry chose the more reserved Gordon Hayes to be his architect. Together, Perry and Hayes created the Oakland Place of the mid-to-late twentieth century.

The first Perry/Hayes building on Oakland Place was a new home erected in 1954 on the former site of 88. This modern traditional house was French rather than Colonial in inspiration; it housed Edward and Miriam Gates, best known for amasing a fortune manufacturing and selling padded brassieres. In the 1960s, Perry made his greatest impact with the creation of the St. Andrew's Walk development. This cluster of high-end row houses maximized land use and catered to those who sought smaller accommodations but did not want to live in apartments. The result was twelve Colonial Revival townhouses that face each other over a quaint pedestrian walkway, each with its own rear garage. This arrangement was a new version of North Street's 1928 Mayfair Lane development. Unfortunately, two grand Oakland Place mansions, 48 and 60, were demolished in 1962 to bring St. Andrew's Walk to fruition.

Perry and Hayes were inspired by the Colonial architecture of Tidewater Virginia, when they collaborated on 21 in 1973. The house, smaller than many on Oakland Place, has a prominent end chimney facing the street. It was the last new house built on Oakland Place. In design, detail, and craftsmanship, it is in keeping with all other homes on the street.

In that time period, just as today, there were people with financial means who had no desire to maintain a large residence. St. Andrew's Walk was one solution. Oakland Place offered other options as well. Seymour Knox began a trend in 1955 when he gutted the interior of 65 and had it rebuilt by Gordon Hayes into a double house, with front and rear units. Some Oakland Place homes had been divided before that time, but this was the first to involve such drastic changes. More divisions followed in the 1960s and 1970s, but most retained some of the original interior elements and generally did not have much effect on the street façades. The result is that, to the casual observer, they still appear to be single-family homes. Given the resurgence of demand for large homes, some Oakland Place houses that had been converted to multiple-unit dwellings have been changed back to their original status as single family homes (2, 103, and 138). The carriage houses behind many of these grand homes were also rebuilt as residences in the years after World War II.

The neighborhood was changing in other ways as well. During the lean years of the Great Depression, the Franklin School on Park Street was consolidated into the Elmwood School on Bryant Street, and the resulting academic institution was named the Elmwood-Franklin School. The old school buildings proved inadequate for the expanding enrollment after World War II. In 1951, the school moved to a new campus designed by Duane Lyman & Associates on New Amsterdam Avenue, adjacent to the Nichols School. The old campus was demolished the following year by Children's Hospital, which was greatly expanding to meet changing heath care needs. In 1953, construction began on a nine-story addition next to the two-story main building, which dated to 1908. The new building, situated perpendicular to the street, appeared from Oakland Place to be a narrow tower, thus maintaining the scale of the street. However, a master plan unveiled in 1968 resulted in a drastic change: the 1908 main building was demolished and replaced with a massive ten-story structure parallel to Bryant Street. Although situating the new structure behind the original two-story building would have mitigated its effect, the concept of integrating the old with the new to create a harmonious whole had not yet arrived in Buffalo. Some of the residents unsuccessfully fought the expansion. The ten-story structure towers over Oakland Place to this day.

In the late 1970s, local residents formed the Summer-Oakland-Bryant Association (SOB) block club to maintain the quality of life in the neighborhood and to foster a positive relationship with Children's Hospital (now Women's and Children's Hospital). They soon realized that the organization's acronym of SOB had negative connotations, so they changed the name to the Bryant-Oakland-Summer Association (BOS). Evidently, some of the residents did not want to be known as SOBs!

Into the Twenty-first Century

Today, Oakland Place remains one of the loveliest and most elegant residential streets in Buffalo. This tranquil thoroughfare retains its charm and continues to be among the city's most desirable addresses, still the "exclusive and unusual little community it has always been." Its impressive streetscape of splendid nineteenth and twentieth century residential architecture promises to delight well into the twenty-first century.

View looking southeast onto Oakland Place
from Women's and Children's Hospital.

PRESENT OWNERS: KEVIN AND SARA FITZPATRICK

2 Oakland Place

This house, which was completed in 1884, is an excellent example of the Stick style of architecture. The horizontal and vertical wood members project slightly above the clapboards and represent underlying structural members; however, these are not actually load-bearing components. The clapboards, vertical flush boarding, and board-and-batten siding provide further variety to the exterior surfaces, as do the incised ornament and decorative verge boards. The composition is capped by a picturesque gable and hip roof with fluted chimneys. The richly detailed front porch was a key element of the design, but it was lost when the entrance was relocated to the side.

185 Summer Street, circa 1901.

The home's interior features an entry leading to an elaborate open staircase with rich Eastlake detail still in its original natural finish. The adjacent living room, or main hall, is a remarkable space. The massive brick and terra cotta fireplace has an oak leaf and acorn motif. A raised frieze with foliage and birds extends around the entire room, and all of the doors and windows have fine Eastlake casings. In the paneled dining room, an Eastlake fireplace features a mantel supported by twin pilasters. Although some of the home's extraordinary detail was lost when the structure was converted to apartments, much still remains.

The home was built for George C. Sweet (1851-1928) and his wife, Ida. His wife was the official property owner, a common practice at the time. Sweet was a principal in J. B. Sweet & Son, which manufactured baby carriages in a factory on Niagara Street. The house was designed in late 1883 by George J. Metzger, a notable local architect, and was completed the following year. At that time, Oakland Place did not exist and the original address of the house was 185 Summer Street. Sweet purchased the lot from his brother-in-law, George L. Lewis. The Lewis home, located next door at 195 Summer Street, had been constructed the previous year. George Metzger had prepared the plans for the Lewis home as well. The Sweets added a carriage house at the rear of the property in 1893. That building is now a separate residence, 18 Oakland Place.

In 1907, Abby W. Grosvenor (pronounced Grov-en-er) purchased the home. She was a relative of Seth Grosvenor, a prominent early resident best known for his bequest to the city to establish a reference library. That library was located in a large building of its own at the corner of Franklin and Edward Streets until the collection was merged into the Buffalo and Erie County Public Library in the early 1960s. The present Grosvenor Room at the Central Library houses the library's genealogy, music, and rare book collections.

Abby Grosvenor lived in the house with her sister, Lucretia, and their nephew, Dr. W. Harry Grosvenor. Ownership of the house passed to Lucretia in 1923 and to Dr. Grosvenor three years later. Although he had been trained as a physician at Johns Hopkins, Dr. Grosvenor eventually chose to work in investment securities rather than in medicine. He died in 1942 and the house was sold to Hugh and Lillian Gregory. The Gregorys divided the house into four apartments in 1949; the current owners are in the process of restoring it to a single-family home.

Details of Eastlake staircase and newel post.

18 Oakland Place

This house was originally built in 1893 as the rear stable of the George and Ida Sweet home at 185 Summer Street (now 2 Oakland Place). In addition to the horses and carriages, the building housed the Sweets' German-born coachman, his wife, and their two children.

The stable was constructed of brick, with the carriage door in the center of the Oakland Place façade. When the Sweets sold their house in 1907, their neighbor at 22 Oakland Place, Mrs. Julia Hill, purchased the stable. She commissioned Esenwein & Johnson, a prestigious local architectural firm, to remodel it into a residence. The work was completed in 1909. The architects created balanced façades of half-timbered double gables with a full second story and attic. The half-timber frame was originally left natural or painted a dark color, the plaster was done in a light color, and the brick was left unpainted. The home is Tudor in style, but the exposed rafters and brackets provide a strong Craftsman feel.

Left: Colonial Revival main staircase. Right: Detail of half-timbered gable.

The home features a grand entry hall that opens into the living and dining room. The centerpiece of the entry hall is a Colonial Revival staircase that sweeps elegantly to the second floor. In addition to built-in window seats, the staircase features newel posts decorated with the stylized triglyphs and guttae that were characteristic of Esenwein & Johnson's work during this period.

After the conversion was complete, Gertrude Francis, widow of leather belt manufacturer William Francis, moved into the house with her family. When Mrs. Francis died in the house in 1928, note of her passing included mention of her home and her beloved books:

> Known to old time comrades as 'Gertie Wilson,' Mrs. Francis was a representative of what was finest and best in a past page of our social history. Her living room or library in Oakland Place was literally book-lined, and what volumes there was not room for in the cases were strewn about on the tables in tempting quantity.

"To One Passing," *Our Record* (Nov. 1928)

At the time of her death, the home passed to her son, insurance agent Gilford Francis; he lived in the house until he sold it to David A. Thompson around 1940. Thompson made alterations to both the interior and exterior in 1947, from designs by Backus, Crane & Love.

Later renovations included the removal of the front porch in 1965, when Edward V. Regan owned the home. Regan is best known for serving as Erie County executive (1971-1978) and comptroller of the State of New York (1978-1993).

Main entry door features a leaded glass window.

21 Oakland Place

Completed in 1973, this is the newest house on Oakland Place. It was designed by architect Gordon Hayes and built by developer Hubert Perry, the team that dominated Oakland Place architecture during the latter half of the twentieth century. Like St. Andrew's Walk, this home reflects Perry's preference for Colonial Virginia as a source of inspiration. This design was modeled on the early colonial houses of Virginia's Tidewater area, whose chimneys were located outside the end wall to reduce interior heat. The result is a rather imposing façade of Flemish bond brick for one of the street's smaller homes. The steeply sloped roof is sheathed in slate and punctuated by small dormers with unusual diagonal siding.

The garage, built at the rear of the house, was converted to a family room in 1987 and a new garage was constructed next to the house. The home's main entrance is along the north side; it opens into a small hall with a staircase that leads up to the dormer-lit second floor. The living room, located to the right of the entrance, extends across the entire width of the house and features a large, raised fireplace and north-facing bay window. The dainty dining room is located next to the entry hall, behind the living room, with the kitchen to the rear.

Mary Goodyear Kenefick (1907-1977) had this house built following the death of her husband, Theodore. Prior to his death, the Keneficks had lived on St. George's Square. The daughter of A. Conger and Mary Forman Goodyear, Mary, or Polly as she was known to her friends, grew up around the corner, at 160 Bryant Street. Her father, who is credited with kindling Seymour Knox's interest in modern art, later moved to New York City and became the first president of the Museum of Modern Art.

The Chinese influenced wallpaper compliments the Federal style furniture in the dining room.

22 Oakland Place

In addition to being one of the oldest houses on the street, 22 Oakland Place is also the street's first architectural transplant. Built circa 1876, the house originally stood at 201 Summer Street. The style was most likely Second Empire, which was ubiquitous during the period. In that style, the home would have been crowned by a mansard roof. The balanced, symmetrical façade, with its very tall, paired windows capped by richly detailed lintels of applied ornament, was also characteristic of the style.

The house was originally occupied by James Haldane, a market gardener who had a business on Michigan Street, a farm at Jefferson and Best Streets, and a large vegetable garden on his Summer Street property. The Haldane property was later purchased by George L. Lewis, a local attorney. In 1890, Lewis moved the house to this location so that he could build a grander home at 197 Summer Street (which now houses the American Cancer Society).

With the move came a new, high hip roof with large Shingle-style dormers on each face; each dormer had a blank shingled arch in the gable. A new flat-roofed porch was also added, extending over two-thirds of the façade, supported by Tuscan columns, and capped by a balustrade. The front dormer also had a small porch and balustrade. The large Palladian window on the stair hall may also have been added at that time. The geometric mullion patterns in this window and the dormer add interest to the façade.

The home's interior retains its original layout. A narrow central stair hall runs from the front to the back, essentially dividing the house into halves. The large living room to the left of the stair hall was originally two rooms from which the partition wall was removed. The elegant dining room occupies the right side of the entrance hall, its original marble fireplace still intact. The kitchen and sun parlor are located to the rear of the dining room.

The earliest resident at 22 Oakland Place was Frederick C. Williams, a grocer who had moved to Buffalo from Massachusetts. He became a partner in Faxon, Williams & Faxon, "which acquired the reputation of being one of the finest grocery, wine, cigar, and imported foodstuff stores in Western New York" ("Chain Store Unit Founder is Dead," *Buffalo*

Above: Dining room from entry hall.
Left: The house circa 1901.

BUFFALO & ERIE COUNTY HISTORICAL SOCIETY

News, March 6, 1935; this obituary refers to the younger Faxon). After Williams died in 1897, attorney Charles B. Hill bought the home and lived there for many years with his wife, Julia. In 1909, Julia Hill had the stable of 18 Oakland Place converted into a residence; in 1910, Hill expanded 22 Oakland Place by augmenting the existing space with a small addition.

Besides his legal practice, Hill took a great interest in the civic affairs of Buffalo. In 1914, when the city of Buffalo implemented a commission form of government, Hill served as one of the first councilmen. His subsequent service included chairing the Upstate Public Service Commission. The family's legacy to the city did not end there. Julia Hill's father, Horace J. Parmelee, was one of the founders of Westminster Presbyterian Church on Delware Avenue.

The demise of Charles Hill was perhaps the most bizarre event in the history of Oakland Place. During a blizzard in February 1927, Hill walked out the front door of his home, headed for the Saturn Club, and vanished. An acquaintance

later reported seeing him walking south along Elmwood Avenue shortly after he left home, but there were no other sightings. His disappearance was front-page news for several weeks, but none of the leads resulted in a solution to his whereabouts. Two months later, Hill's body was found floating in the barge canal at the foot of Massachusetts Avenue. He may have become disoriented and somehow fallen into the canal during the storm, but the exact circumstances of his death were never discovered. Julia Hill continued to live in the house after her husband's death. She died there in 1943 at the age of 88.

Elbridge S. Sidway, whose father lived a few doors down at 38, purchased the house following Julia Hill's death. In the early 1950s, Sidway sold the house to attorney John P. Wickser. The Wicksers added a family room at the rear of the house in 1976.

27 Oakland Place

This fine Colonial Revival home has been greatly simplified from its original appearance. It was built in 1896 by Loverin & Whelan, an architectural firm best known for apartment houses, most notably the Lenox on North Street.

The house, four bays wide, was originally fronted by a porch that extended across three-quarters of the façade. Slender Ionic columns supported the porch and the balustrade above it. When the porch was removed after World War II, the present simplified classical entry, including the door with concentric squares, was installed. The windows feature eight-over-one sash, and thin corner pilasters frame the façade. Numerous pedimented dormers containing arched windows line the hipped roof. The windows' upper sashes are composed of intersecting arched mullions. An ornate railing with a geometric pattern originally linked these dormers. Unfortunately, as the

The Federal style living room mantel was brought here by a previous owner from a house on Lexington Avenue.

Joseph Dudley. Charlotte and Alfred Wright moved to the Lenox Apartments on North Street and died in 1906 within two months of each other.

Joseph G. Dudley (1869-1949) lived in the house with his wife, Angeline Moon. A native of Minnesota, Dudley moved to Buffalo in 1893 and, before passing the bar two years later, clerked for Ansley Wilcox (in whose Delaware Avenue house Theodore Roosevelt was inaugurated as President). Dudley, whose career spanned fifty-four years, was considered one of the city's best legal minds. His firm's last incarnation was Dudley, Stowe & Sawyer. Prominent in local society, Dudley served as president of the Buffalo Club, dean of the Saturn Club, and vice president of the Buffalo Country Club.

After World War II, industrialist Clinton R. Wycoff, Jr. and his wife, Dorothy Knox Goodyear, purchased 27 Oakland Place. They had lived briefly at 130 on the other end of Oakland Place. Clinton's parents lived across the street at 48 and Dorothy's uncle, Seymour Knox, lived at 57. Wycoff was an officer with the Atlas Steel Castings Company; when his father died in 1947, Wycoff succeeded him as president. The Wycoffs removed the porch and modified the interior in 1946, and the house was later divided into front and back units.

wooden details deteriorated, they were removed rather than repaired. The bays along the south side of the house were added in the 1980s.

The interior arrangement is unusual for a Colonial Revival home. The entry is at the northwest corner and the entry hall follows an exterior wall. (This arrangement is also used at 29, 33, and 62 Oakland Place.) The paneled vestibule leads to a small paneled hallway that runs along the north side to the staircase, the home's most dramatic interior feature. The landing projects beyond the exterior wall, and the window is capped by a fanlight of delicate leaded glass. The Colonial fireplace with its beautiful detail highlights the wainscoted living room. Not original to this house, the fireplace was installed by owners who moved it from their previous home on Lexington Avenue. The elegant dining room features a fireplace with simple detail that was likely added after World War II.

The house was commissioned by Charlotte Wright as a home for herself and her husband, Alfred P. Wright (1833-1906). Born in Oswego, Alfred settled in Buffalo in 1866 and prospered in businesses associated with the Erie Canal. The Wrights did not live in their new home for very long. They sold it around 1904 to attorney

Circa 1901.

28 Oakland Place

This fine house has had only three owners. It was designed in 1901 by the distinguished firm of Lansing & Beierl and its construction was well supervised by architect Williams Lansing, who lived across the street at 29. A substantial brick house that completely fills the narrow lot, the home was described as an Elizabethan cottage when it was new. Prominent twin front gables with finial-capped parapets and massive end chimneys that rise above the parapet-framed red tile roof balance the asymmetrical façade. The unusual brickwork in the chimneys gives the impression of multiple freestanding flues. The large bay trimmed with stone on the left side of the house is played off against the windows to the right, which have stone sills and lintels with drip moldings. The Flemish bond brickwork is only on the front, and the striking contrast between the red stretchers and glazed black headers has faded with time.

The home is an unusual combination of medieval exterior and Colonial Revival interior. Perhaps Lansing wanted his view to include a medieval house across the street, while the owners decided that the Colonial Revival style was more suitable for the interior.

The house under construction. *Brickbuilder* (July 1902)   BUFFALO & ERIE COUNTY PUBLIC LIBRARY

Elegantly detailed Colonial Revival main staircase.

The entrance originally included a semicircular porch supported by Tuscan columns; the ghost of this porch can still be discerned on the façade. The tiled vestibule of this Tudor house includes a hidden interior treasure in the form of a fine Federal doorway complete with leaded sidelights and a fanlight. A small flight of stairs leads to a stair hall that divides the house, in true Colonial fashion, into halves. The staircase offers a straight flight to the second floor and features an unusual newel post with a twisted Baroque column, topped with an Egyptian capital. This eclectic combination is faintly echoed in the thin balusters of both the front and back staircases.

Pocket doors frame the entry hall and all the doorframes have ears, meaning that they extend outward at the top. The den, on the right side of the hall, was redone in full-height paneling in the 1950s. The living room opens off the left side of the hall. It is original and features a bay window, built-in bookshelves, and a fine fireplace with paired Tuscan pilasters. A Cupid baby grand piano that once belonged to Josephine Shea, wife of theater magnate Michael Shea, is another highlight of this room. The dining room, which is located at the rear of the house, features a fireplace with Ionic columns and a band of windows with an exceptional view of the back yard. The rear

Above: The tastefully furnished living room is brightly lit by the large bay window.

Right: The pantry retains the original cabinetry.

staircase is as impressive as the one in front. Open from the basement to the attic, it is characterized by delicate spindle work.

The house was built for John A. Mann (1857-1949) and his wife Elizabeth Churchyard. A descendent of one of the city's pioneering families, Mann didn't attend college, but joined the workforce after high school. (During that time, few people attended high school, let alone college; there was in fact only one high school in Buffalo until 1895.) He entered the linseed oil business in 1882 and was president of Mann Bros. Co. on Ohio Street when this house was built. Mann died in this house in 1949. His first wife had died in 1918, and in 1926 Mann married her niece, Charlotte Churchyard. After his death, his widow sold the house to lawyer Robert and Eleanor Millonzi, who lived here until 1971. Millonzi is best known for his extensive contributions to the Buffalo Philharmonic Orchestra. In fact, the location of the Orchestra's former administrative offices, Millonzi House, bore his name. His daughter Molly was later chief of protocol for President Bill Clinton.

Left: The wide living room fireplace features an austere mantel supported by twin engaged Tuscan columns flanking a marble surround with ears.

Far left: Detail of dining room fireplace, showing engaged Ionic column and classical detailing.

Below: Egyptian capital of main staircase newel.

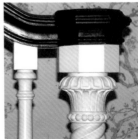

29 Oakland Place

Mary Lansing purchased the lot at 29 in 1897, and her husband, Williams Lansing, a principal in the architectural firm of Lansing & Beierl, designed a home for the propery. This house has the distinction of being one of only two on the street built as an architect's home.

Lansing made maximum use of the narrow lot by designing two adjacent homes separated by a thick party wall. Together, 29 and 33 Oakland Place presented a balanced and unified façade. The façades and floor plans of these Colonial Revival residences were originally mirror images. Bays fronted the living rooms, which were situated under the master bedrooms. Although the entrances originally included front porches supported by smooth Tuscan columns, only the porch at 29 remains. The windows are nine-over-nine sash, and a Palladian window on each side highlights the main staircases. Balustrades originally topped the high hip roof with its flaring eaves and the area between the dormers. The thick party wall is topped by a massive center chimney.

The vestibule leads to an entry hall with an exquisite Colonial staircase that turns twice as it ascends to the second floor. The hall opens directly into a large living room. A fireplace with Tuscan columns is flanked by built-in bookcases, while a large bay window overlooks Oakland Place. Pocket doors lead to the dining room that features the original beamed ceiling. The ceiling in the living room matches the dining room, but it is not original; it was added by one of the home's later owners. A triple window, overlooking the back yard, is framed by leaded glass bookcases on either side. The first floor of this home also features pedimented casings on all of the door and window openings; this unusual feature suggests an appreciation of Greek Revival architecture.

Williams Lansing (1860-1920) had worked for several years as a clerk before joining the architectural office of Green & Wicks in 1886. He opened his own office in 1889 and began a partnership with another former Green & Wicks draftsman, Max G. Beierl (rhymes with spiral), three years later. Lansing & Beierl soon became one of the leading architectural firms in Buffalo. The firm designed a variety of buildings, including the massive Connecticut Street Armory and a series of imposing churches, beginning with the Lafayette Presbyterian Church. They also excelled at residential design, as evidenced by at least five homes on Oakland Place (28, 29, 33, 37 and 127). In 1910, the firm became Lansing, Bley & Lyman. Lansing's partner Duane Lyman later built his own house at 78.

The Lansings moved to Bryant Street in 1914 and sold their home to Norman and Margaret Clement, who were living in the adjoining 33. They intended to turn the two homes into one. Upon learning that major structural complications would result, they instead rented out 29 to Bert L. Jones, general manager of the spectacular Niagara Gorge Railway. In 1919, Clement sold both 29 and 33 Oakland Place to his brother Harold T. Clement (1890-1971). A 1912 graduate of Yale, Harold was treasurer of the Rogers-Brown Iron Company. He and his wife, Constance, lived in 29 and rented 33 to another brother, Stuart H. Clement. (The Clement brothers' mother lived directly behind at 786 Delaware Avenue, now the American Red Cross.) In 1923, the Clements sold both 29 and 33 and moved down the street to 116.

Katherine Cooke Brehm was the next owner of 29. She later married Preston B. Porter and, in 1929, sold the house to an industrialist named Cecil W. Farrar. Farrar was president of Excelso Products Corporation, a company that manufactured water heaters. He eventually became president of the Case Manufacturing Company before retiring to Florida. In 1945, he sold the house to Louis C. Dodd, who lived in the house until his death in 1960. Harold T. Clement's namesake son, who lived here as a child, purchased the house in 1965, so at least one Oakland Place resident seems to have proven that you can go home again!

JOAN & NORMAN EFFMAN

Above: View of dining room during the Clement ownership, circa 1920.

Below: The living room has fine views into tree-lined Oakland Place.

32 Oakland Place

This house is a magnificent example of the Shingle style, possibly the best example of the style on the street. All exterior surfaces, including the roof, were originally unified through the use of wood shingles as the sole material. The entire structure seems to grow out of the ground and the battered base enhances that effect. The integrated tower, in turn, appears to grow out of the composition while the brick chimney, which is exposed on the first story, disappears into the body of the house before bursting through the roof. In addition to these features, the exterior has many of the more subtle details associated with the style, such as the saw-tooth shingles above the windows, the tiny blank openings at the top of the tower, symbolizing dovecotes, and the arrow slits at the top of the side gable.

An inviting front porch originally graced the façade. Although it is gone, the house's greatest treasure remains inside: a magnificent spindle staircase that winds up to the second floor. The newels have Romanesque details and classical caps. The delicately turned spindles, with whimsical patterns of beading throughout, are simply a joy. The staircase also features a built-in seat located at the base, and a large triple window, composed of numerous small panes of clear glass leaded in intricate geometric patterns, highlights the landing. The living room, located to the right of the entrance, appears to have been remodeled in the 1920s or later. It features an elegant classical fireplace and diamond-pane casement windows. The leaded transoms above the windows are original.

Clarissa F. Griffin, widow of John F. Griffin, commissioned the house early in 1890, but she died in July of that year, at age 57, before it was finished. Her daughter Sarah saw the house to completion and sold it in 1891 to Frances E. Beecher (1855-1919). Miss Beecher was one of the street's most interesting residents and a good example of how individual involvement contributed to making this community. It was later remembered that:

Circa 1901 view of the home with original porch.

> **Miss Beecher was one of the guiding spirits of the Oakland community, her zeal in keeping it up to its self-appointed level of elegance often bringing her into collision with some luckless parvenu or cheeky contractor who sought to edge into the sacrosanct confines. Any day she was to be seen, driving hither and yon in her small phaeton buggy, drawn by what was perhaps the most famous horse in the city, yclept Gladys. This steed, a rather hard-boiled sorrel mare with a banged tail and a rolling eye, had been one of the Cary's polo ponies in her salad days and now, broken to carriage harness, she yet expressed her contempt for mere man-made rule by deliberately taking and keeping the center of the road at all times. Except when a policeman hove into sight. Then Gladys is said to have accepted discretion as the better part, and turned right dutifully.**
>
> "Oakland Place Cow Out O'Luck 25 Years Ago," *Buffalo Express* (March 14, 1926)

Fannie Beecher kept her horse and buggy long after everyone else on the street took up the automobile. When Gladys died around 1915, Fannie buried the

horse with her harness, destroyed the buggy, and never bought another horse.

Miss Beecher's brother, attorney James C. Beecher (1840-1915), also lived at 32 Oakland Place. He was known for presenting an annual Fourth of July fireworks display for the neighboring children, occasionally sharing the expense with neighbor Frederick Truscott (33).

After Miss Beecher's death in 1919, the house was purchased by William A. Griffin (1882-1942), president of the North Buffalo Hardware Foundry. It is possible that Griffin was related to the original owner. Griffin lived in the house for a few years before acquiring a grander house on the street through an interesting set of circumstances. Around World War I, Trinity Episcopal Church was bequeathed a mansion on Delaware Avenue across from the church for use as a rectory. Church officials thought the mansion was too large, so they sold it and purchased 80 Oakland Place with the proceeds. It was later decided that this home was also too large. The result was a trade: William Griffin moved to 80 Oakland Place and his home at 32 Oakland Place became the rectory for Trinity Episcopal Church. Dr. Cameron J. Davis (1873-1952), rector of the church since 1901, lived here until he was named bishop in 1930. His successors occupied the house until 1969, when the church sold the house, and it again became a private residence.

The beautifully detailed spindle staircase is one of the finest on Oakland Place.

33 Oakland Place

This is the northern half of a Colonial Revival double house. Bessie Sweet Truscott (1862-1941) purchased the lot early in 1897, around the same time that Mary Lansing purchased the adjacent lot. Mary's husband, Williams Lansing, a principal in the architectural firm of Lansing & Beierl, maximized the use of available space by designing a double house containing a residence on each lot.

Although a thick party wall divided the two residences, 29 and 33 Oakland Place presented a balanced and unified façade. The façades and floor plans of these Colonial Revival residences were originally mirror images. Large bays mark the location of the living rooms and master bedrooms. Although the entrances originally included front porches supported by smooth Tuscan columns, the porch on 33 Oakland Place was removed by one of the home's later owners. The windows are nine-over-nine sash, and a Palladian window on each side highlights the main staircase. Balustrades originally topped the high hip roof with its flaring eaves and the area between the dormers. The thick party wall is topped by a massive center chimney.

BUFFALO & ERIE COUNTY HISTORICAL SOCIETY
This duplex home, shown circa 1901, contains both 29 and 33 Oakland Place.

The Colonial Revival living room mantel, decorated with urns and pendant bellflowers.

The interior, which originally mirrored the interior of 29, retains the Colonial staircase with its Palladian window. The living room is in the front and the dining room is behind it. All of the door and window openings are framed by pedimented Greek Revival casings. In the early part of the twentieth century, 33 was expanded. Instead of windows at the east end of the dining room, a short stairway leads down to a rich and inviting library. This room has a beamed ceiling, wood-mantel fireplace, built-in bookcases, and walls covered in oil paper.

When the house was completed, Bessie moved in with her husband, Frederick Truscott (1863-1922). Frederick was a prominent member of Buffalo's social scene, and his professional life included work as a grain merchant, officer at a safe deposit company, and electrical contractor. Around 1907, the Truscotts rented the house to Langdon Albright, the son of prominent industrialist John J. Albright. In 1910, Bessie Truscott sold the house to Norman P. Clement (1885-1951) and his wife, Margaret.

Around 1912, the Albrights moved out and Norman and Margaret Clement moved in. (The Albrights later settled at 120.) After graduating from Yale in 1907, Norman Clement had begun working for the Marine Bank, where his father, Stephen M. Clement, was president. Norman became the bank's cashier in 1913 and was one of the incorporators of the Federal Reserve Bank the following year. The rear of Norman's property abutted the grounds of his mother's grand home at 786 Delaware Avenue. (His father had died in early 1913, just months before the mansion was finished.) One of the benefits of this arrangement for Norman was the use of his mother's garage. Mrs. Clement's Delaware Avenue mansion currently houses the local branch of the American Red Cross.

In 1914, the Norman Clements purchased 29 Oakland Place with the intention of combining 29 and 33 into one grand residence. They soon discovered that

The master bedroom.

The elegance of formal dining is preserved on Oakland Place.

Recently remodeled kitchen features an inlayed floor.

breaching the thick party wall would be a tremendous undertaking so they built an addition onto 33 instead, completing this work in 1916. Three years later, Norman's brother, Harold T. Clement, and his wife, Constance, purchased both residences and lived in 29. They rented 33 to another brother, Stuart H. Clement. Stuart was the cashier of the McConnell Grain Corp. The three brothers were quite familiar with this area. In their early years, they had lived at 173 Summer Street, at the end of Oakland Place.

The Clements sold 33 in 1923 to Proctor Carr, vice president in charge of sales at Buffalo Bolt Company. He added a garage for his cars in 1923 and further expanded the house with an addition in 1927. After his death in 1936, his wife, Susan Ward Carr, kept the house until 1944, when she sold it to Mrs. Winifred Smith Mathewson. The house has changed hands several times since then, and the various owners have made a variety of minor changes, of which removal of the front porch is the most significant.

37 Oakland Place

This is Oakland Place's most effervescent rendition of the Colonial Revival style. A full-width porch supported by fluted Tuscan columns fronts the balanced façade, while, on the second story, oriels flank a pair of oval windows. The high hip roof is pierced by numerous dormers, each topped with broken swan's neck pediments and finials, and the roofline was originally crowned with a balustrade. The north façade is especially interesting: delicate oriel windows of curved leaded glass flank the massive chimney. The projecting second floor shelters them and enfolds the chimney. In a departure from the usual clapboards, the entire exterior is clad in alternating wide and narrow bands of shingles.

The paneled, double vestibule is an unusual feature; to the right of it is a small room that can serve as a sitting room or reception room. The paneled stair hall is straight ahead from the vestibule. The staircase rises past a large leaded glass Palladian window to the open second floor hall. The delicate Colonial balustrade bears a natural finish; the entire hall originally had the same finish. The door and window casings have ears, or slight projections of the lintels, and the bottoms of the door casings have returns, which are very unusual.

A large library lies opposite the stairs. This room has built-in bookshelves, leaded glass windows, and a beautiful Gothic fireplace detailed with slender columns, quatrefoils, pendants, and rosettes. A small office next to the library contains a built-in desk. This was a good location for the butler to manage the house. The elegant dining room which also boasts leaded glass windows, opens onto the stair hall to the east. Adjacent to the dining room is a small breakfast room overlooking the yard.

The home was built for William H. Hotchkiss and his wife, Katherine Bush. It was designed in late 1897 by the firm of Lansing & Beierl, and work was completed the following year. Katherine's family lived in a mansion at the northwest corner

TOM AND LAURA CHESTNUT

Circa 1901 view of the home; note the original gas street light.

An unusual gothic fireplace dominates the library.

of Delaware Avenue and Summer Street, and they had owned the land on which this new home was built since 1860, long before Oakland Place was established. Hotchkiss was a lawyer with Hotchkiss & Bush, and he later served as state superintendent of insurance. William and Katherine sold the house in 1904. They moved to a new home, also designed by Lansing & Beierl, at 20 Lincoln Parkway.

Frank St. John Sidway (1869-1938) purchased the house from them, and it remained in his family for more than 70 years. Sidway was a descendent of three of the most prominent and wealthy families of nineteenth-century Buffalo: St. John, Spaulding, and Sidway. The St. John family's history in Buffalo included the fact that the family homestead was the only one spared by the British when they burned Buffalo in 1813. Frank's grandfather was United States Representative Elbridge Gerry Spaulding, who introduced legislation to create the first Federal paper money during the Civil War. The currency was known as the greenback; the tradition continues today as American paper money has been printed with green backs ever since.

Frank eventually assumed the role of the family's patriarch. As a symbol of his prominence in the family, portraits of his grandparents, Jonathan and Parnell Sidway, hung on either side of the dining room window. In addition, a famous painting by Thomas LeClear, *Interior with Portraits,* was hung in a place of prominence above the fireplace in the library. The 1865 painting, which features two of Frank's relatives, now hangs in the Smithsonian.

Frank St. John Sidway was a prominent lawyer who had practiced in the city since graduating from the Buffalo Law School in 1894. He took a leave during law school to fight in the Spanish-American War. In addition to practicing law, Frank managed estate investments and the interests of the Sidway family. The family's holdings included the Sidway Building at Main and Goodell Streets.

The breakfast room has a fine view into the backyard.

Frank's brother lived across the street at 38, and his nephew Elbridge later lived at 22. When Frank St. John Sidway died in 1938, ownership of the house passed to his wife, Amelia Roberts Sidway, who lived in the house for another forty-four years. A descendant remembered that on the eve of World War II, servants still served all meals in the dining room. To summon them, Mrs. Sidway simply had to step on a button in the floor beneath the table. Just before her death in 1972, ownership of the house passed to her daughter Edith, who lived here with her husband, Steven I. Stevens, until 1975.

Circa 1901.

PRESENT OWNER: RICHARD NEAL

38 Oakland Place

Built in early 1890 for Henry J. Pierce (1857-1947) and his wife, Violetta, this is one of the first homes completed on Oakland Place. Pierce was president of the Buffalo Alcholene Company, which was located at Fourth and Pennsylvania Streets. It was later called the Manhattan Spirit Company, and finally, the Wood Products Company, and was one of the largest producers of wood alcohol in the nation.

As constructed, the house was a grand example of Shingle style architecture. Massive triangular gables beneath a steeply pitched roof projected above the bays of the second floor. The first floor boasted a wide veranda and a porte cochère framed by wide shingled arches. Exterior details were limited, with the exception of carved triangular panels in the gables. The design relied on the effect created by the shape, massing, and texture of the shingled surfaces. This subtle effect has since been hidden under vinyl siding. The original transom windows on the first two stories of this home are unique, composed of small leaded panes and edged in bands of blue and yellow opalescent glass.

When the Pierces moved to a new home on Summer Street in 1895, they sold 38 to Maud L. Porter. She lived in the house with her new husband, Alexander J. Porter (1863-1932). A member of the pioneering Porter family of Niagara Falls, Alexander was a prominent banker and industrialist. He later served as president of the Shredded Wheat Company of Niagara Falls.

In 1907, Charlotte Spaulding Sidway, matriarch of one of the most prominent families of Buffalo's social scene, purchased 38 Oakland Place as a home for her son, Clarence S. Sidway (1877-1953), and his wife, Genevieve Hingston (1880-1939). Clarence and Genevieve lived near several family members, including Clarence's brother across the street at 37 and Genevieve's parents and sister at 88. Their son, Elbridge, later lived at 22.

Clarence graduated from Cornell University in 1897. He served as secretary-treasurer of the Robertson-Cataract Electric Company for

Portion of semicircular railing at second floor landing is one of the few original details that remain in the house.

more than fifty years. (That company's building still stands at the corner of West Mohawk Street and South Elmwood Avenue.) When his mother died in 1934, ownership of the home transferred to two of Clarence's brothers and he purchased it from them. He continued to live at 38 Oakland Place until his death, in the house, in 1953. The following year, his second wife, Claire Collins Sidway, converted the house into two units: one in the front and one in the back. She sold the house in 1964.

In addition to Claire Collins Sidway's remodel in 1954, the house was remodeled again in the mid-1960s. The result is that most of the original interior details of this home have been lost.

St. Andrew's Walk 48-60 Oakland Place

St. Andrew's Walk is a small community within a community that echoes the dignity and elegance of Oakland Place. It was originally the site of two of the grandest mansions on Oakland Place. Both mansions were designed by C.D. Swan, a virtuoso of residential architecture. The homes at 197 and 210 Summer Street are remaining examples of his work.

A towering house with a golden Roman brick exterior was built at 48 Oakland Place in 1892. A porch made from stone and terra cotta graced the entire width of the front, and bays and turrets projected from the sides of the house. A steeply pitched tiled roof pierced by dormers and a row of chimneys, each with a separate tile roof, completed the home's exterior.

The mansion was built for Louis Schoellkopf (1855-1901). Louis was a principal in J.F. Schoellkopf's Sons, tanners and cut sole manufacturers. His father was "King Jacob" Schoellkopf, a German immigrant and industrialist whose company was the first to harness the power of Niagara Falls. Following the death of Louis in 1901, his widow, Myra Horton, continued to live in the house until her death in 1910. The house was subsequently occupied for an extended period by Clinton R. Wycoff (1874-1947). A leading local industrialist, Wycoff founded the Atlas Steel Castings Company and served as its president for many years. His son and namesake, who succeeded him as president, lived across the street at 27. Wycoff's widow, Emma, later moved to 87 Oakland Place. The Charles H. Hyde and Manley Fleischmann families were the last to occupy this home.

The massive house at 60 Oakland Place was designed in 1891 and built for tanner James Horton, who was most likely the brother-in-law of Louis Schoelkopf of 48. The home's exterior sheathing of rough-faced Medina sandstone initially gave it a distinctly Richardsonian appearance. That impression was lost to view, however, as vines from the foundation to the tops of the towering gables gradually covered the house.

James N. Adam (1842-1912) purchased the home around 1895. A native of Scotland, Adam came to Buffalo on the advice of his brother, Robert B. Adam, a founder of the Adam, Meldrum & Anderson department store (AM&A's). James founded his own store, J. N. Adam & Co., in 1881. The store was so successful that a ten-building complex was eventually built to house it at Main and Eagle Streets. (That complex became AM&A's in 1960. It is still standing, but its future is in jeopardy.) In 1906, about the time he entered politics, Adam sold

48 Oakland Place in its last days. Photo taken by Lois M. Fleischmann, 1962.

The vine-covered 60 Oakland Place. *Beautiful Homes of Buffalo* (1915)

the company that bore his name, and was elected mayor of Buffalo three times, serving from 1906 until 1909. After Adam's death, Harry D. Williams (1862-1952), a prominent local lawyer, purchased the home and occupied it for the rest of his life.

It does not appear that the architecture of this house was appreciated in its time. One neighbor later recalled 60 Oakland Place as being dark and forbidding, both inside and out.

In the early 1960s, developer Hugh Perry decided to replace these homes, which were then considered to be anachronistic Victorian dinosaurs, with a new housing development. Perry's work was well known among the denizens of Oakland Place; in fact, he is credited with changing the face of this Buffalo street during the mid-to-late twentieth century. The mansions at 48 and 60 were demolished in 1962, but the two-story stable behind 48 was left standing. This 1907 building remains today, converted into a residence.

Following the demolitions, new construction began immediately. Although Perry had originally intended to build three or four freestanding homes around a courtyard, he soon discarded this plan in favor of one that involved twelve upscale row houses facing each other over a stone walkway. The name of this quaint pedestrian thoroughfare became the name of the development: St. Andrew's Walk. Inspired by the architecture of Colonial Williamsburg, Perry instructed his architect, Gordon Hayes, to design the façades in the Georgian style. The red brick composition, common to all the homes, provides a harmonious appearance, but subtle differences in treatment make each home's exterior unique. These differences also led to the idea that the residences were built over an extended period of time, rather than within several years of each other. Two of the homes front Oakland Place, and the one at 60 is unique among its St. Andrew's Walk neighbors for its gambrel roof. In a marked departure from Colonial precedent, the others have flat roofs.

Each home has its own terrace behind a brick wall that undulates along the walk. In addition, built-in garages are accessible from driveways at the rear of the homes. The development was not built all at once; rather, the homes were constructed individually as the lots were sold. The first was completed in 1963 and the last was finished by 1970. Perry and Hayes worked with the owner of each home to design a customized Colonial interior. The result is that no two homes are alike but they share common elements, such as fireplaces, elegant open staircases, and simple, tasteful moldings. Numerous notables have called St. Andrew's

Walk home over the years. Irvine Kittinger, treasurer of Kittinger Furniture lived in one of the homes, as did Haskell Stovroff, noted Buffalo industrialist; attorney Lawrence R. Goodyear; banker Robert M. Schue; and Calvin G. Rand, co-founder of the Shaw Festival. Another original owner is Marion Osborne, daughter of Alex Osborn, who was founder and CEO of Batten Barton Durstein & Osborn, one of the world's most renowned advertising companies. Guests of Seymour Knox also had the opportunity to experience life on St. Andrew's Walk because he purchased one of the homes to serve as his guest quarters.

Present owners include: Mr. and Mrs. Robert J. A. Irwin (6); Mrs. Irvine J. Kittinger, Jr. (10); Mrs. Haskell I. Stovroff (11); Marion Osborn (14); Mr. and Mrs. James How (15); Calvin G. Rand (16); Mr. and Mrs. Robert M. Greene (17); Professors Murray and Adeline Levine (18); Anne G. Keating (21); and Dr. and Mrs. Philip C. Moudy (22) on St. Andrew's Walk, and Mrs. Craig L. Benjamin (48) and Mr. and Mrs. Richard F. Griffin (60) on Oakland Place.

60 is one of two homes on St. Andrew's Walk that face onto Oakland Place.

The tastefully furnished living room in 10 St.
Andrew's Walk features a simple yet elegant
Colonial staircase leading to an open landing.

57 Oakland Place

This is one of the largest homes on Oakland Place, befitting the merchant prince who lived here for over six decades, millionaire philanthropist Seymour Knox.

Construction began on this magnificent Georgian Revival mansion in 1924, the year after Seymour married Helen Northrup. Construction was completed the following year, and the Knoxes moved into their new home, a gift from Seymour's mother. The architect is unknown, but was possibly C. P. H. Gilbert of New York City, who had designed the Knox mansion at 800 Delaware Avenue a few years earlier. Seymour and Helen's first home was a massive Georgian Revival design rendered in Flemish bond brick. It presents a balanced façade to the street and the eye is drawn to the great central Palladian window of the staircase. Small round-roof dormers pierce the low hip roof, which is sheathed with slate that becomes smaller and thinner towards the top. Massive chimneys with quoins and arches anchor the entire composition. A unique cornice of coved brackets above fret molding adds visual and architectural interest.

The living room during Seymour Knox's later years.

AVERY KNOX

The main entrance, accessible through a stone porch supported by freestanding Ionic columns on the north side, faces an auto turnaround and a sunken garden. A tunnel-like vine arbor leads to the door from the street. The house features a magnificent series of rooms, many of which overlook the gardens behind the house. The L-shaped main hall leads to a grand staircase that has a slender balustrade of steel and brass. Under the large Palladian window, the staircase curves gracefully upward to the second floor. Beyond the hall is the large, elegant dining room. An exquisite marble fireplace, with simple, classical ornamentation embellishes this room whose ceiling is made of exquisitely detailed plaster with a large oval medallion in the center. Separated from the dining room by a removable steel and glass screen, the breakfast room has French doors that open onto the garden terrace. The large ballroom, located in the basement, was the location for many grand Buffalo society functions.

Nicknamed "Shorty" in reference to his diminutive stature, Seymour H. Knox, Jr. (1898-1990), one of Buffalo's wealthiest and most influential citizens for most of the twentieth century, had a "giant" impact on his city. He was the only son of Seymour H. Knox, Sr., who partnered with his cousin Frank W. Woolworth in pioneering the 5-and-10-cent store. The senior Knox later established a chain of similar stores, known as S. H. Knox & Company. When the chain merged into F. W. Woolworth & Company in 1912, Knox became vice president. A fellow Woolworth official, Elbert S. Bennett, lived at 110. With his great fortune, the senior Knox moved into banking, but he died unexpectedly in 1915 at the age of 54.

Seymour Jr. thus came into a vast inheritance at a very young age. He proved to be very adept financially. As a result of his skill, the family fortune grew tremendously. In addition to managing the family finances, he served as a director of numerous local and national companies. Most notably, he was the longtime chairman of Marine Midland Bank. During his tenure, he was the principal force behind the construction of the bank's new office tower in Buffalo. That structure, which straddles lower Main Street, is still Buffalo's tallest building. It now houses HSBC Bank, the international banking company that purchased Marine Midland Bank.

Though Knox excelled at business, modern art was his great passion. A. Conger Goodyear, who lived around the corner from Knox at 160 Bryant Street, sparked Knox's interest shortly after Seymour and Helen moved onto Oakland Place. Although Goodyear later moved to New York City and became the first president of the Museum of Modern Art, Knox's passion for modern art never

Circa 1930.

waned. Knox purchased millions of dollars worth of art for the Albright Art Gallery over the years; his dedication and generosity were pivotal in making it into one of the nation's leading venues for modern art. He donated most of the money for a new wing to the Gallery in 1962; when it was completed, the Gallery was renamed the Albright-Knox Art Gallery in recognition and appreciation of the importance of his leadership and generosity.

Knox was also an enthusiastic sportsman whose skill made him one of the top polo players in the nation. He led his team to a national championship in 1932. He shared his passion for sports with his two sons and their enthusiasm resulted in the creation of the Buffalo Sabres, the city's team in the National Hockey League (NHL).

The Knox family lived in great style. The family's fortune enabled them to enjoy luxuries such as a household staff even when servants were rare in other homes on Oakland Place. Just before the start of World War II, for example, 57 Oakland Place was home to eleven people, including servants. In addition to this grand mansion, the family enjoyed their residences in East Aurora, approximately 20 miles from Buffalo, and Aiken, South Carolina.

A portrait of Seymour Knox, Sr., gazes down from the paneled wall in his son's library at 57 (1973).

The walls of the Knox home were lined with numerous examples of artwork drawn from his extensive collection, as in this 1973 bedroom view.

A view up the driveway into the gardens of 57 Oakland Place. The Wilson house (61) formerly stood at left. The stables that comprise the present 61 Oakland Place are just beyond.

61 Oakland Place

This is the site of the shortest-lived mansion on Oakland Place. It was designed in late 1901, completed in 1903, and demolished two decades later. This was also the only residence on Oakland Place designed from the ground up by the prestigious architectural firm of Esenwein & Johnson.

The home was constructed of iron-spotted Roman brick in tones ranging from warm brown to yellow brown; this is the same material used on the home Frank Lloyd Wright designed for Darwin D. Martin on Jewett Parkway. In addition to a large front porch, the house had an open-air loggia that faced south and overlooked the property on which 57 was later built. The house was capped with a low-pitched hip roof of terra cotta tile that was pierced by tall chimneys with their own tile roofs, similar to the chimneys across the street at 48. Most of the windows had slightly pointed arches, a very unusual feature. The home defies easy stylistic categorization, but the heavy shadows cast by the widely overhanging roof were said to be in the Italian spirit. The house at 781 West Ferry Street, designed by Esenwein & Johnson at the same time, also has similar details and features. It allows one to get a sense of the character of the manse that once stood at 61.

This house was commissioned by Mrs. Margaret L. Wilson, who remained in the home until her death in 1919. She was the widow of Robert P. Wilson, an attorney and veteran of the Civil War. Her adopted son, Charles R. Wilson, lived with his wife, Mabel Letchworth, at 95. After Margaret's death, George W. Mixter lived at 61 Oakland Place. Mixter was president of the Pierce Arrow Motor Car Company, which produced some of the nation's most distinguished automobiles.

Around 1924, Mrs. Seymour H. Knox, Sr., evidently acquired the property, which bordered her grand Delaware Avenue estate to the east. She was in the midst of plans to build a house for her son on the vacant lot to the south (57) and it appears she wanted to build a similar house for one of her daughters at 61 Oakland Place. The twenty-year old home was demolished, but plans for the new house never materialized and the site eventually became a sunken garden north of the Knox mansion. The stable was retained as the garage for 57, but it was significantly altered to better match 57's Georgian design: the yellow brick was painted red and a parapet replaced the extensive overhang of the roof. In addition to the former Wilson stable, the property also now includes the former stable of the Knox mansion on Delaware Avenue. Both buildings contain elegant apartments.

The long–vanished Wilson house. *The House Beautiful* (July 1904)
BUFFALO & ERIE COUNTY HISTORICAL SOCIETY

The original appearance of the Wilson stable. *Brickbuilder* (July 1902)
BUFFALO & ERIE COUNTY PUBLIC LIBRARY

Present owners: Don Borowiak (62); Dennis and Cindy Greco (64)

64 Oakland Place

This is the first Colonial Revival home to be built on Oakland Place and one of the earliest examples of the style built in Buffalo. It was designed in the fall of 1890 and completed the following year. The rectangular house was sheathed in dark clapboards, and the surrounding trim was painted in white or a light color; it must have been a striking sight in a city of Queen Anne and Shingle style homes painted entirely in dark earth tones.

The flat-roofed round tower projecting from the south side is a holdover from the Queen Anne style. Five doric columns with egg and dart capitals support the inviting full-width front porch, which was originally topped by a delicate balustrade with finial-capped newels. Above it, two large oriel windows flank a small oval window with four long, thin keystones. The high hip roof features a Palladian front dormer and the rooftop, dormer, and tower were all originally crowned by dainty balustrades.

An unusual Dutch door with leaded sidelights opens to a long, wainscoted double vestibule lit by leaded glass. The vestibule leads into a magnificent main hall that features a grand staircase, a large paneled fireplace, and a beamed ceiling. The staircase is one of the most dramatic on the street: the stairs cascade down from behind a triple-arched arcade supported by Ionic columns with egg and dart molding in the capitals. A large U-shaped seat, built into the wide landing, sits beneath a pair of windows with lunettes of green, red, and orange opalescent glass. The original den, located at the south end of the hall within the tower, was converted into a kitchen. It is accessed through a tall arch supported

Circa 1901.

BUFFALO & ERIE COUNTY HISTORICAL SOCIETY

The beamed ceiling and an unusual interior arcade highlight the impressive main hall.

by Ionic columns; a screen with upside-down balusters similar to those on the staircase flank the arch.

A paneled fireplace, topped by a triple arcade of Tuscan pilasters with sunbursts in the arches, is a focal point in the parlor. This exquisite fireplace also has a lovely curio shelf with spindle supports. The original dining room, which is skirted with cherry wainscoting, features a corner fireplace with a fire back of flaming torches.

The home was built for Margaret Shortiss, who lived here with her daughter, Marguerite, and new son-in-law, Frank W. Fiske (1866-1949). Originally from Albany, Margaret moved to Buffalo shortly after her daughter's marriage. Frank Fiske was an independent insurance underwriter who joined E. C. Roth & Company the year he moved onto Oakland Place. His boss, Edward C. Roth, became a resident of 102 around the same time. Fiske formed the Armstrong-Roth-Cady Company in 1907, eventually becaming its president.

With Margaret's death in 1901, title to the property passed to Marguerite. She and Frank continued to live in the house, and the title passed to him when she died in their home in 1939. Frank remained in the house until his death ten years later. The house was then purchased by Joseph Rittling and his wife, Diane, who lived there until 1976. Rittling was vice president and treasurer of the Rittling Corporation, which manufactured a wide variety of heating units. The single-family home was converted to two units (62 and 64), one in the front and one in the back, by the owners who acquired it in 1976. The gambrel-roofed stable at the rear of the property has also been converted into a dwelling with the address of 66.

65 Oakland Place

Balanced and symmetrical, this grand five-bay Colonial Revival manse hits all the high notes of the style. It was constructed in 1895 of buff-colored Roman brick, with stone sills and splayed lintels, though the house is now painted. An especially rich cornice extends around the building. The cornice has elegantly molded leafy modillions interspersed with coffered rosettes separated by a row of dentils from a band of torches, swags, and wreaths. It is surely one of the most original cornices to grace any home in the city. The house has a high hip roof pierced by a pair of towering paneled chimneys and numerous dormers with alternating triangular and rounded pediments. The central element of the façade is the original rectangular porch, with a semicircular projection, which, supported by six Ionic columns, extends over the curved stairway. The porch balustrade is a replica of the original and was installed around 2000.

The residents of this home welcomed guests at the entry door, which featured leaded sidelights and a leaded transom. The paneled entry vestibule with a beautiful mosaic floor led into the main hall with its lovely beamed ceiling. An elegant staircase on the north side gracefully curved up to the second floor and

Circa 1954.   BUFFALO & ERIE COUNTY HISTORICAL SOCIETY

there was a small office to the left of the entrance. The main hall opened at the south end into a substantial living room that featured a curved bay window, built-in bookcases, and a fireplace in a corner nook. The main hall also led to the formal dining room, which had a dainty fireplace. The enclosed sun porch was located beyond the dining room. Portraits of venerable ancestors were hung throughout the home, and a tall case clock kept time in the main hall.

The house was built for Henry Ware Sprague (1855-1932), one of the most prominent attorneys in the state, and his wife, Mary Noyes. After studying at the University of Leipzig in Germany, Sprague joined his father's legal office and passed the bar in 1879. His early law partners included John Milburn, president of the Pan-American Exposition, and Norris Morey (107). An ardent reformer, Sprague served as chairman of the Buffalo Civil Service Reform Commission. After his death, it was noted that he made the Pan-American Exposition possible by chairing the committee that raised more than $1,000,000 in one week. His brother Carleton, one of the directors of the exposition, was also a prominent citizen. The Saturn Club was founded in his home, and he served as its first dean. Their sister was married to the prominent New York architect Walter Cook; it is likely that Cook's firm, Babb, Cook & Willard, designed the house. This firm designed Carleton's home (which is now gone) on West Ferry Street, as well as several structures for the Pan-American Exposition. When

The elegant entry portico features a recently restored balustrade.

Henry Sprague died in his home in 1932, his strong character was noted:

Few men have endeared themselves more universally. A quick impatience, followed quickly by a disarming smile, won more friendships than if he had been apathetic. He had the salt of humor which kept him sane and had also a sweetness of spirit which expressed itself in generous service both to his city and to his friends. "Henry W. Sprague Represented Character and Citizenship in Buffalo," *Buffalo Evening News,* (April 21, 1932)

Sprague's wife, Mary (1863-1954), was a longtime member of the Garret Club and of the Children's Hospital Board of Managers. She was described as "charming and cultured in the social graces all her life" ("Mrs. H. W. Sprague, Old-Family Member, Dies in 65-Year Home," *Buffalo News*, April 2, 1954). A further description noted that the youthful Mary Noyes "was as brilliant as she was lovely to look at. She had the most luxuriant brown curly hair, an irresistible smile, and was one of the most popular girls in that coterie of charming young women" ("The Duchess Strolls Pomander Walk," *Buffalo Courier*, Feb. 27, 1934). Vice President Theodore Roosevelt was among the guests Mary welcomed to 65 Oakland Place. She was later said to have recalled, "He was bright, charming, a bit boisterous … and spilled red wine all over my dining room floor!" Mrs. Sprague continued to live in the house for twenty-two years after her husband's death until her own until her own death in 1954.

Seymour Knox (57) subsequently purchased the house, in 1954, to protect his adjacent property. Knox retained architect Gordon Hayes to convert the house

into front and rear units in 1955. During this renovation, the interior was gutted and restrained Colonial interiors were installed in keeping with the time. Only the entry vestibule remained unaltered. Ruth Wickwire, widow of industrialist Ward Wickwire, moved into the front unit (her son had briefly occupied 130), while Knox's namesake son, Seymour III, occupied the back.

Opposite and above: Three views showing the original appearance of the home's beautiful interiors—living room (left), dining room (center), and entry hall (right)—which were lost when the house was gutted and remodeled in 1955.

Right: A view of the exterior's richly detailed frieze and cornice.

70 Oakland Place

Elegant design, exquisite detail, and a unique roofline distinguish this exceptional Georgian style residence. Designed by Boughton & Johnson, it was commissioned in late 1896 and completed the following year. William H. Boughton (whose first independent commission was at 103) cited this house as one of three examples of his design ability when he applied to join the American Institute of Architects (AIA) in 1899. James A. Johnson, Boughton's partner, left Boughton & Johnson to form the prominent firm of Esenwein & Johnson not long after this house was completed.

This substantial brick house, perhaps the finest designed during the Boughton & Johnson partnership, is characterized by a symmetrical five-bay façade, a projecting entry bay capped by a pediment, and corners defined by fluted Ionic pilasters. Marble lintels above the windows are unusually well detailed. The front door has delicate leaded sidelights and a fanlight. The second-floor doorway to the porch roof is framed by Ionic pilasters and leaded sidelights. The equally refined side entrance is beneath a gracefully curved roof supported by Ionic columns, which originally extended out to form a porte cochère.

An unusual feature of this home is its flat, rather than the traditional pitched, roof. A recessed third floor, covered in shingles and framed by pilasters, rises from it, creating a terrace that extends around the roof's entire perimeter.

Architect Edgar Allen Poe Newcomb made alterations to the house for the second owners in 1913. A subsequent remodeling by Esenwein & Johnson in 1923 included a new dining room addition. A 1965 appraisal of the home yielded this description of the interior:

On the first floor there is a large center hall, a reception room, a side entrance with port cochère, flanked by a guest closet, lavatory and basement stairway. There is a large living room with a woodburning fireplace, beam ceiling and built-in bookcases. A one-story addition in the rear has a very large dining room with a marble fireplace, wainscoting with scenic wallpaper and service closet; a large library with woodburing fireplace, beam ceiling and built in bookcases. In the service wing there is a maid's sitting room, a large kitchen and butler's pantries with large cabinets and built-in Jewett refrigerator.

This interior was substantially altered when the home was converted to three units in 1968 but many fine details remain. The beautiful front door now leads out onto a secluded porch and some of the fine fireplaces are intact. Above the side entrance, the spectacular elliptical open staircase with square balusters winds its way up through three floors. On the landing, freestanding Ionic columns frame a sash window with its own leaded sidelights and fanlight.

This home was built for Robert W. Pomeroy (1868-1935) and his wife, Lucy Bemis. A native of Auburn, Pomeroy graduated from Yale and Harvard Law School before coming to Buffalo to begin his legal career around 1895. If the grandeur of his home is any indication, business was booming from the beginning. His practice turned increasingly to finance and Pomeroy soon became one of the city's leading financiers. After fifteen years in this home, Robert and Lucy moved to a new estate just over the city line in Amherst. When they moved to New York City to be closer to the center of the financial world on Wall Street, their Amherst estate became the subdivision of Pomeroy Park.

Lavinia Avery Mitchell purchased the house from the Pomeroys in 1911. Her husband, James McCormick Mitchell (1873-1948), was the son of Reverend Samuel S. Mitchell. James moved to Buffalo in 1880 when Reverend Mitchell became pastor of the First Presbyterian Church. A graduate of Princeton and the Buffalo Law School, James was one of the area's leading lawyers and a principal in the firm of Kenefick, Cooke, Mitchell & Bass. One of his colleagues, Lyman M. Bass, also lived on Oakland Place, at 129.

Mitchell specialized in tax claims and he succeeded in getting one Buffalo business a momentous $10,000,000 refund after World War I. His success extended to the social scene, where he served as president of the Buffalo Club, the Buffalo Country Club, and the Tennis and Squash Club, as well as dean of the Saturn Club. Lavinia Mitchell continued living in the house for nearly twenty years after his death. She is best known for selling her late mother's mansion to the city of Buffalo in 1938 to serve as the site of Kleinhans Music Hall.

Lavinia Mitchell sold the Oakland Place house to developer Hugh Perry in 1967. The following year he divided it into three units: front, middle, and rear. He accomplished this by inserting party walls and a new side entrance, as well as undertaking significant remodeling, especially in the middle unit. Perry also converted the rear stable into three units and called the complex Blackfriars Lane. All of the units were purchased soon after completion.

Present owners: J. P. Losman (70); David and Ginger Maiman (72); Edward and Ceil Linder (74).

Circa 1901. <small>BUFFALO & ERIE COUNTY HISTORICAL SOCIETY</small>

A view up the elegant spiral staircase.

77 Oakland Place

Although the first home on Oakland Place originally stood here, this site is better known as the home of Buffalo's Roman Catholic bishops during the last half century.

The original mansion was designed by Charles F. Ward and built circa 1888, on a wide lot, soon after Oakland Place was created. Queen Anne in style, the first story was stone with frame construction above. A wide porte cochère on the north side was balanced by a large porch with an octagonal roof on the south side. The third story featured projecting gables, and a large tower dominated the south elevation. The house was built for William D. Olmsted (1842-1924) and his wife, Mary Olive Matthews. A prominent industrialist, Olmsted had moved to Buffalo from New York in 1878. He worked in the flour-milling firm of Schoellkopf & Matthews. (George B. Matthews lived at 830 Delaware Avenue directly behind the Olmsteds.) Olmsted later served as president of the Niagara Falls Milling Company. He was also connected with the Niagara Falls Power Company, a major supplier of electrical power formed by "King Jacob" Schoellkopf and George B. Matthews. (Schoellkopf's son Louis lived across the street at 48.) William lived in the house at 77 until his death. In 1927 his widow sold the mansion to Georgia M. G. Forman, who demolished it to make way for an even grander home.

A native of Lockport, Georgia M. Greene (1871-1955) had married Howard A. Forman (1870-1931) in 1892. Howard's father, George V. Forman of 824 Delaware Avenue, had made a tremendous fortune in the oilfields of northern Pennsylvania. Howard was vice president of the Eastern Oil Company and later succeeded his father as president. Howard's brother, George, was worth $5,000,000 when he died in 1925, and it is likely that Howard's fortune was similar. However, Howard was evidently not the most faithful of spouses, and he and Georgia separated around 1920; Georgia was obviously very well settled.

After living modestly on North Street, Georgia commissioned her new home from the prominent firm of "Edward B. Green & Sons – Albert Hart Hopkins" in 1927. The grand Tudor manor house of random cut limestone was completed the following year. The principal façade, which is almost symmetrical, hints at E. B. Green's classical predisposition, as do the Ionic volutes atop the finials flanking the entrance bay. The composition is anchored by four massive stone chimneys that soar above the roof. The slates on the roof, which get progressively smaller and thinner as they rise, add to the perception of height. The metal gutters and collectors are unusually well detailed. In keeping with the medieval flavor of the design, leaded casement windows are used throughout the home.

An open Gothic arch on the north side leads to the stone garage that has space for five automobiles on the first floor and an apartment above. The garage's residential quarters, which are accessible via a spiral staircase in a tower, were originally occupied by Mrs. Forman's son, Lawrence, and his wife, Jane Weed. The residential quarters bear a separate address of 81 Oakland Place. The house and apartment share splendid views of the grounds, including the garden terrace and substantial back yard.

The grand home's entry vestibule, which has walls of stone and a diamond-patterned coffered ceiling, provides a foretaste of the splendor to come. The entryway leads to a main hall built on two levels: a small staircase with delicate iron railings passes beneath a Gothic arch supported by stone columns on the way to the hall proper. A carved frieze surrounds the room under a pitched coffered ceiling. Pointed arch doorways open onto the home's other principal rooms, including a loggia with fine views of the terrace garden. The staircase, in contrast

A circa 1901 view of 79 Oakland Place, the first house built on the street, which was demolished for the present 77.

BUFFALO & ERIE COUNTY HISTORICAL SOCIETY

Left: Entry hall with coffered ceiling and subdued staircase.
Top: Detail of dining room ceiling, showing hand-painted ornamentation.
Bottom: The elegant study features full-height wood paneling.

to those in many other homes on Oakland Place, is small and tucked into a corner. It denotes the more private nature of the upstairs rooms.

To the south off the main hall, the library extends the entire depth of the house. The centerpiece is a large stone fireplace with carved paneling above, and all of the walls feature tall built-in bookcases. Large casement windows at either end of the room have transoms with antique stained glass roundels, and carved heads project from the central doors. The plaster ceiling, done in geometric relief with Tudor detail and a grape vine border, is the most elaborate on Oakland Place.

A study is located at the opposite end of the hall. It is a cozy classical room with floor-to-ceiling wood paneling in a natural finish. A marble fireplace is located at one end of the small room; it has a lovely carved wood surround of flowers, swags, and a fruit basket. A semicircular niche with shelves graces the opposite wall.

In contrast to the medieval flavor of the library and hall, the dining room is classically detailed. It features an elaborate black and white marble fireplace supported by pilasters, with a small, carved relief wolf and stork drinking from a vase. The beautiful plaster ceiling includes a border of painted fruit; the ceiling's other details are highlighted in gold. The pantry, original cabinetry intact, is located beyond the dining room and is larger than many kitchens. It leads to a kitchen that retains its original ceramic tile walls, range hood, and built-in Jewett refrigerator.

At the end of 1952, when Mrs. Forman was in her 80s, she moved into the Campanile Apartments and sold her home to the Catholic Church. The new Roman Catholic Bishop of Buffalo, Joseph A. Burke, had decided that the location of the Episcopal palace on Delaware Avenue, in front of the Blessed Sacrament Chapel, had become too noisy with traffic. The diocese therefore purchased the Forman mansion on tranquil Oakland Place, and it is there that the Roman Catholic bishops of the Diocese of Buffalo have lived for more than half a century.

This comment appeared in Mrs. Forman's obituary; "Her house was a meeting place for distinguished men and women from this city and abroad." Even today, an opportunity to visit 77 Oakland Place is not to be missed.

Above: View of gardens showing rear of house and turreted stable. Right: Detail in carved door panel.

78 Oakland Place

This gem of a house, designed by one of Buffalo's leading architects as his own residence, is the second to be built on the site. The first was erected in 1893 in the Queen Anne style and bore the number 80. Characterized by a high hip roof, tall corner tower, and a full-width front porch, the house was built for William Anderson, a native of Scotland who came to Buffalo in 1867 and co-founded the Adam, Meldrum & Anderson department store (AM&A's). Although Anderson's partners did not live on Oakland Place, some of their family members did. James Adam, Robert Adam's brother, lived at 60, and Herbert Meldrum, son of Alexander Meldrum, lived at 88. It is interesting to note that both of these Oakland Place denizens operated competing department stores.

Anderson's time in his new home was short-lived; he succumbed to heart disease in 1897, at age 67. Two years after his death, his heirs sold the home to George A. Plimpton, a principal in Plimpton, Cowan & Company, wholesale druggists and grocers. When Plimpton died in 1911, ownership of the house passed to his widow, Jenny.

In 1919, Jenny Plimpton sold the home to Trinity Episcopal Church. Although a house had been bequeathed opposite the church on Delaware Avenue, it was deemed too large for use as a rectory. Church officials felt that 80 Oakland Place might be more suitable, but it also proved to be too large. In 1924, the rector chose a smaller house at 32 Oakland Place. This transaction was evidently a trade, as the occupant of 32, William A. Griffin, moved into 80. An industrialist, Griffin served as president of the North Buffalo Hardware Foundry and vice-president of the Standard Foundry. He spent most of the rest of his life in the house, but it was demolished in late 1940, shortly before his death.

The 1893 stable, with its unusual dormers capped by pointed polygonal roofs, was spared from demolition. In 1949, it was split off from the main property and retained the address of 80 Oakland Place. For several years, it was the home of B. Mason Bowen and his wife, Jean. Bowen was a realtor with Gurney, Overturf & Becker; in 1953 the Bowens purchased 123.

Built-in cupboard in corner of living room.

Architect Duane Lyman (1886-1966) constructed his new Georgian style home on the front portion of the lot in 1949-1950. Lyman had been among the first Buffalonians to move to Amherst. In fact, he built his home there in 1912 on a street he named after himself! When the exodus from Buffalo to the suburbs began in earnest after World War II, he bucked the trend by moving back into the city. Lyman built one of the smallest homes on Oakland Place, and it is said that he built a small home to forestall the possibility that his children (and their children) could move into the house.

The house is as elegant and well built as the other homes on Oakland Place. The beautifully detailed entrance is the focal point of the three-bay façade of Flemish bond brick. The refined entrance features twin engaged columns flanking a solid door, capped by a fanlight set in a marble arch. The delicately leaded oval windows on either side of the doorway add to the grace and beauty of this entry. The adjacent first floor windows are set in arches, and the second floor is defined by incised limestone belt courses. The house is topped by a flat roof with a brick parapet and open grillwork.

Inside, the staircase rises perpendicular to the front door in the tightly structured entry hall. To the left, the paneled living room features a fine colonial fireplace, built-in bookshelves, and corner shelves with rib-arched semi domes. Lyman designed the living room to be the principal interior space, and rather than creating a separate dining room, he incorporated a dining alcove at the west end. This alcove provides a lovely view of the terrace and yard through a curved bay window. The adjacent kitchen features the original cabinetry.

Duane Lyman was considered the dean of Buffalo architects at the time of his move to Oakland Place. Over the years, he was a principal in Lansing, Bley & Lyman, then Bley & Lyman, and finally Duane Lyman & Associates. His firms designed many of the finest office buildings, schools, churches, and residences in Western New York. After Lyman's death in 1966, his wife continued to reside in the house until 1974.

87 Oakland Place

This restrained example of Colonial Revival style was constructed in 1916 of dark red brick with a hipped slate roof. The house is unusual in that exterior architectural features are alluded to by subtle variations in the brickwork and trim rather than being overtly expressed. At the corners of the house, straight vertical mortar joints extending through both stories suggest pilasters, and abstract details in the cornice give hints of capitals. There are small stone blocks below slightly raised vertical projections in the frieze, and a dentil course above in the soffit that appears only at the corners. Small stone blocks at the foundation also serve to suggest pilaster bases. The windows have brick lintels, while two of those on the first-story front are enhanced by semicircular arches of flush brick. These windows originally flanked a small front porch. Trelliswork inserted between the slender paired columns echoed the arched tops of the windows. The driveway extended back to the garage along the north side of the house, past the principal entry, which was beneath a large round roof supported by freestanding Tuscan columns.

87 Oakland Place, circa 1930, with original entrance on north side.
Buffalo, The City Beautiful: Its Homes, Gardens and Environs (1931)

A small vestibule led into the main hall, where a grand staircase with a large leaded glass window dominated the south end. To the right, a large living room extended across the full width of the house, and the dining room was located to the left of the entrance. The pantry and kitchen were located beyond the dining room. All the principal rooms in the house have at least two exposures.

The house was built for lumberman George A. Jackson (1863-1928) and his wife, Claire Truitt. The architectural firm of Wood & Bradney designed the house; this firm had also designed the adjacent house at 95 in 1913. An officer in the lumber and cooperage firm of Jackson & Tindle, George Jackson had joined the firm in 1898, becoming secretary and treasurer in 1917. His appointment as secretary and treasurer roughly coincided with the Jacksons' move into their new home. At the time of his death, Jackson was vice president of the Buffalo Council of Churches. His funeral was held from his Oakland Place home, and his executors subsequently sold the house in 1928 to industrialist Eugene J. McCarthy (1869-1929) and his wife, Mabel.

A native of Auburn, McCarthy came to Buffalo around 1890 and went to work as a salesman for Beals & Company, manufacturers of steel and heavy hardware. He eventually worked his way up to become president of the firm, which became Beals, McCarthy & Rogers. (Harold T. Clement, of 29 and 116, had been treasurer of the predecessor firm, Rogers-Brown Iron Company.) In addition, McCarthy was vice president of McCarthy Bros. & Ford, electrical contractors. McCarthy did not get to enjoy his new home for very long: he died of a heart attack in the home at the age of 61. His death occurred in early 1929, less than a year after he and Mabel had purchased the property.

In 1932, Mabel McCarthy significantly modified the residence she had shared with her husband. In addition to moving the main entrance and driveway from the north to the south side, she had a new flagstone terrace installed on the shady north side. A new entry vestibule with a concave copper roof was constructed on the south side; the result was that people entered the main hall from beneath the grand staircase. Full-height paneling was installed in the large living room and the cozy library upstairs, and a substantial fireplace of green marble surrounding a bronze frame was installed in the living room.

At the same time, Mabel demolished the original garage and built a new brick garage and studio for her daughter, Lucy. This building features a garage door on the right side of the first story and a large pedimented entry bay rising two stories. The rest of the second story is contained within an unusually prominent Mansard roof. As with many slate roofs of the period, the individual slates get smaller and thinner towards the roofline. On the first floor, a family room,

91 Oakland Place.
PRESENT OWNER: SUSAN NUSBAUM

Above: Simple detailing and wood paneling characterize the living room of 91 Oakland Place.

Left: A carved marble fireplace is the focal point of the grand living room of 87 Oakland Place.

with a fireplace framed with blue and white Delft tiles, leads out to a garden terrace overlooking the large yard. Well-furnished living quarters are located upstairs, including a large, fully paneled living room with a fireplace, a dining room containing built-in corner shelves with seashell motifs, and a conservatory that has been expanded into a bathroom. The new home was designated as 91 Oakland Place.

Mabel McCarthy was able to enjoy the renovations for only two years, as she died in 1934. The property passed to Lucy, who had recently married H. Leibee Wheeler, treasurer of the investment securities firm of Hall, Cherry, Wheeler & Company. The newlyweds moved into 87 and rented 91 to real estate agent Henry D. Lanctot and his wife. After World War II, H. Leibee Wheeler and Lucy parted ways. He moved into 91 and Arthur M. Young, an engineer with Bell Aircraft

Corporation, rented 87. Emma Wycoff, widow of Clinton R. Wycoff, who had previously lived at 48, subsequently rented 87. Her son lived at 27. In the 1950s, Lucy married Charles Caldwell, the legendary Princeton football coach. About the same time, she transferred the property to her son, William Wheeler. In 1959, William sold both houses to David and Rita Leopold. David was vice president of WEBR, a local radio station that broadcast from a former mansion at 23 North Street. Rita was the daughter of William J. Connors, publisher of the Courier Express. The Leopolds lived in 91, and in 1961 they sold 87 to Guy Owens, a physician at Roswell Park Memorial Institute, and his wife, Janet.

88 Oakland Place

It is said that 88 Oakland Place is the house that was built by padded brassieres. This cube-like residence was built for two of Oakland Place's most interesting residents: underwear designer Miriam Gates and her husband, Edward.

Theirs was not the first home built on the site. Its predecessor was a large front-gabled Queen Anne style house with a stone first floor and clapboards above. A flight of stone steps led up to the full-width front porch supported by bulbous columns that continued northward beyond the porch to form the porte cochère. There was a large bay with curved glass windows on the north side and oriels on second floor, one of which wrapped around a corner. The original house was constructed in 1891 for dredging contractor Edward J. Hingston (1844-1924) and his wife, Mary (1851-1928). Charles F. Ward was the architect.

The Hingstons transferred the house to their daughter, Louise Meldrum, in 1907. Their other daughter, Genevieve Sidway, lived at 38. Louise's husband, Herbert A. Meldrum (1870-1960), was the son of Alexander Meldrum, a partner in Adam, Meldrum & Anderson (AM&A's), but rather than join his father's department store, Herbert began his own. H. A. Meldrum & Company was one of the leading department stores in the city for more than three decades. The firm went out of existence in the early 1920s, but the name is still faintly visible on the north façade of its one surviving building at 265 Pearl Street, which was designed by Lansing & Beierl in 1909.

In 1906, Meldrum hired a balloon to take him up over the city as a publicity stunt for the store. During the flight, he took the first aerial photographs of Buffalo. Meldrum was also one of the organizers of the local Automobile Club in 1899, and later served as national president of the American Automobile Association (AAA). In addition, he had the distinction of owning the first commercial truck in the city.

The original grand house at 88 Oakland Place was demolished in 1940. *Beautiful Homes of Buffalo* (1915)

In 1928, the home was sold to Roger R. Hayes and his wife, Winifred Hall Hayes. Roger was a dealer in investment securities, but he was not immune to the destructive force of the Great Depression: title to the house went to the Buffalo Savings Bank in 1933. The bank demolished the home (but not the stable) in 1940 and sold the property two years later to Horace Reed, who lived next door at 94. The Reeds subsequently sold it to Dean and Dorothy Hill in 1952, and the Hills engaged Backus, Crane & Love to remodel the stable into their residence in 1955.

In 1954, the front section of the lot was sold to Edward E. Gates, Jr. and his wife, Miriam. They immediately constructed a new home with a contemporary design inspired by French manor houses. The impersonal Modernism that dominated business and institutional buildings at that time was seldom used for private homes.

Quoins at the corners frame the cubic three-story brick body, which is capped by a simple cornice and slate Mansard roof. The two-story service wing at the rear also has a Mansard roof. French doors and windows are crisply cut into the planar surfaces, and the doors surrounding the first floor lead out to small iron balconies. Three small panels with swags between the first and second floor fenestration are the only applied exterior decoration. Approached from the south, the main entry is through a classically detailed double door that has a small stained glass oculus over it and niches on either side.

Inside the house, the entry leads to a gently curving staircase with brass railings, supported by wrought-iron balusters as it rises past a fireplace to the second floor. The door casings feature bundles of reeds, symbolizing strength, a motif carried throughout the house. The living room, which spans the entire width of the house, features a Baroque fireplace and five sets of French doors leading out to small balconies.

This home was the first of many Oakland Place collaborations for developer Hugh Perry and architect Gordon Hayes. Their clients for this project had one

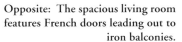
Opposite: The spacious living room features French doors leading out to iron balconies.

Above: Close-up of the exquisitely detailed main entrance doors.

Right: An elegant staircase curves upwards to the landing in the two-story entry hall.

of the most unusual businesses in the city. Miriam Gates was the originator of the padded brassiere, commonly called "falsies." After the end of World War II, Miriam convinced her husband Ed not to resume his brokerage business (he owned a seat on the New York Stock Exchange), but to instead manufacture one of the many product designs she had come up with. The product they chose was the brassiere filled with white foam rubber, designed "to complement the contour of the too-slender girl or woman," surmising that it would not be subject to changes in fashion. This proved to be a superb strategic decision. The business soon became international in scope and expanded every year. Miriam Gates's advertisements became staples in all the women's magazines, and she acquired the nickname of "Falsie" Gates, at least locally. Miriam and Ed lived at 88 Oakland Place until 1970, when they sold the house to Jesse Ketchum, a member of another locally prominent family.

94 Oakland Place

The Horace Reed house at 94 Oakland place is a freely rendered example of the Colonial Revival style, which was very popular in the mid-1890s. This substantial two-story house features an entry porch with Ionic columns. The porch covers only half the width of the house to allow more light to enter the first floor. Numerous bays and oriels project from the rectangular body of the home. The first story is constructed of buff-colored Roman brick with raised mortar joints. The original color is still visible at the chimney tops, but the rest of the brickwork was painted years ago. Subtle features of the first story include a battered base and elongated brick flat arches above the windows instead of the usual lintels. The second story is constructed of clapboards that gently flare out at the top of the first story. The oriels exhibit fine detailing, and the small brackets form a dentil course under the eaves. The hipped roof with flaring eaves is punctuated by numerous dormers with the same flaring rooflines; towering chimneys visually anchor the entire composition.

Buffalo, The City Beautiful: Its Homes, Gardens and Environs (1931)

The orioles feature delicate classical detailing.

The front door, which opens into a vestibule with a beautiful mosaic floor, leads to the stair hall, from which all of the home's principal rooms append. The detailing in the stair hall is Gothic, and it is most pronounced in the foliate-carved newels and tracery-like balustrade. The reception room, located just off the entrance to the stair hall, is the exquisite jewel of the house. It is richly embellished with dainty Corinthian pilasters and other delicate neoclassical woodwork. The grand living room, which is dominated by a large hearth, and the luxurious mahogany dining room also flank the stair hall. The library, with its white oak-beamed ceiling, was added to the house in 1913 and is located beyond the dining room. The upper sashes of the windows throughout the house are made of clear glass and delicate neoclassical leading, and feature a different design in each room.

The house was built in 1894 for John J. McWilliams. McWilliams was the western sales agent for the Delaware, Lackawanna & Western Railroad Company. He had the house built as a wedding gift for his daughter, Mary, and her husband, Horace Reed. A native of Ohio, Reed had come to Buffalo to attend the Bryant & Stratton Business College; he then became the private secretary to William P. Northrup, a prominent local businessman. By 1900, the Reed household had grown to include three sons. With two female servants also living in the house, space was tight so the house was extended to the rear in 1913. The centerpiece of the addition was a large room known as the library, which was also used as a dining room for formal occasions. At one such event, a later hostess had a little fun with her guests: when the cover of the main course was removed, a live duck emerged and waddled across the dinner table. The dinner guests were shocked and delighted by this surprise.

Soon after moving into his new home, Horace Reed joined with his father-in-law and several other men to found the Niagara Lithograph Company in 1896. Reed was initially secretary and treasurer. He became president when McWilliams died in 1912, and served in that capacity for more than forty years. The 1903 factory (designed by Lansing & Beierl) still stands at 1050 Niagara Street. After Reed's death in 1960, 94 Oakland Place was purchased by another Niagara Street businessman, George H. Hyde, vice president and treasurer of the Mentholatum Company.

Opposite, left: Elegant architectural details, such as upper sash of leaded glass, compliment the tasteful decor. Upper right: The substantial library was added to the rear of the house in 1913. Lower right: Rich colors characterize the formal dining room.

This page, left: The main staircase is distinguished by the use of Gothic detailing. The ornate newel capital is especially notable.

Right: A Dutch door with leaded glass in the dining room is a delightfully unusual feature.

95 Oakland Place

Although many of the fine homes on Oakland Place are set on narrow lots, this Tudor style home occupies one of the widest lots on the street. The asymmetrical house is large, yet simply detailed; planar brick walls of Flemish bond are pierced by single sash windows, and bands of casement windows are set in stone openings. A half-timbered staircase bay projects over the north side entry, and further half-timbering runs along the rear façade, giving the impression of a building constructed over time. The front entrance is through a solid panel door with wide sidelights, beneath a narrow entry porch set in a projecting bay with a gabled parapet.

There is no vestibule. The front door opens directly into a large entry hall. The grand staircase faces away from the entrance, which is beneath the landing, and features octagonal balusters connected by pointed-arch moldings. The principal rooms open off the entry hall. A small library, with built-in bookcases and leaded glass windows, is located to the right of the entry hall. Beyond the library is the large living room, which is dominated by a massive fireplace with red marble surround and a mantel supported by Gothic modillions. This room offers fine views of both the front and back yards. The dining room has low wainscoting, a beamed ceiling, and a fireplace of large sandstone blocks and octagonal columns echoing those on the staircase. A doorway leads to an enclosed porch with a brick floor and beamed ceiling. This home also boasts a rathskeller in the basement.

The overall treatment of the interior is fresh and original, a credit to the skill of the locally prominent architects Wood & Bradney, who designed the home in 1913. This project was contemporaneous with their completion of Larkland, the Larkin family compound located along Lincoln Parkway and Windsor Avenue. The Larkins (founder and heirs of the phenomenally successful Larkin Soap Company) had chosen the Colonial Revival designs of Wood & Bradney over the plans of Frank Lloyd Wright, despite the best efforts of Darwin Martin on Wright's behalf. Three years later, Wood & Bradney also designed the adjacent house at 87.

The client for this home was Mabel Letchworth Wilson. The only daughter of Josiah and Katherine Letchworth, Mabel lived here with her husband,

Smooth octagonal columns are the most notable feature of the dining room fireplace.

Charles R. Wilson (1863-1951). Born Charles Winslow in Dorchester, Massachusetts, he was adopted as a child by his mother's cousin, Robert P. Wilson of Buffalo. His adoptive mother, Margaret Wilson, lived at 61 Oakland Place, which has since been demolished. Charles Wilson studied law in his father's office and passed the bar in 1889; after his father's death in 1892, he formed the firm of Wilson & Smith. After his own death, the house was sold in 1952 to William J. McGennis and his wife, Winifred. McGennis served as vice president of the Viking Tool & Steel Company, and he and Winifred lived in the house until 1969.

A vine-free view of 95 Oakland Place, circa 1950.

BUFFALO & ERIE COUNTY HISTORICAL SOCIETY

100 Oakland Place

This Shingle style house has undergone the most radical exterior transformation on Oakland Place. As originally built in 1891, it was a fantastic juxtaposition of projecting and recessed shingled elements. There was a broad semicircular veranda in front of the recessed entry, topped by a delicate balustrade. To the right, an oriel projected above the stone foundation; a large shingled gable had a Palladian window in the center. The shingles above were laid in concentric semicircles with a slender "keystone" under a tiny arrow-slit of a window. At the left of the gable, the front wall was recessed beneath a segmental arch flanked by shingled brackets, and the roof was pierced by a hip-roofed dormer with flaring eaves. The high cross-gable roof was unusual: the north half changed pitch slightly to form a gambrel; the south half was straight. This disparate, but well-designed, composition was effectively unified through the use of wood shingles on all exterior surfaces, including the roof.

After World War II (primarily because of wood deterioration and significant lack of maintenance by the prior owners during the war years), new owners greatly simplified the front façade, removing the porch, flattening out its surfaces into one plane, and even adding flagstone siding. Subsequent owners have somewhat mitigated the effects of the remodeling by restoring the shingle surfaces and adding the small shingled front porch and second floor oriel. Although the polygonal dormer appears old, it actually dates from this later remodeling. The side elevations were little affected by the changes to the front: the tall, shingled bay on the north side and the brick and stone chimney that disappears into the third story on the south are original.

The interior has been significantly altered, which is to be expected given the repositioning of exterior walls. The columned entry hall of amber oak has retained its cross-

after high school, and he compensated by traveling widely and reading voraciously. He was delighted when people asked him which college he had attended. Although he was a wealthy man, Dunston regularly rode his bicycle from Oakland Place to his downtown business. According to legend, he was known for reading a newspaper during the ride! He also invested in real estate: Dunston Street, off Kenmore Avenue, is named for him. Early in the twentieth century, Dunston lost his fortune, partially due to real estate miscalculations. He chose Dunkirk, New York, as a likely place to make a new start, but died before he could recover any of his fortune. His wife, Nellie, continued to live at 100 until her death around 1941. After a court battle between the heirs, the house was sold in 1942 to James Porter (1911-1994) and his wife, Ann (1910-1993). Porter was a lawyer and property manager. James and Ann owned the house until 1968, when it was purchased by their son, Henry M. Porter, a Buffalo attorney, and his wife, Patty.

The reoriented main staircase still retains its original elements.

beamed ceiling, while the fireplace is flanked by small windows with geometrically patterned leaded glass. The door and window lintels feature delicate swag ornamentation. The staircase is composed of its original elements, but it has been reoriented from its original position. A small playroom across from the staircase is situated between the living room and the room that is now the kitchen; the playroom originally contained large glass cabinets.

This house was constructed in 1891 for Bright C. Taber (1861-1926), president of the Taber Pump Company and a prominent tanner. His obituary referred to him as a "pioneer in the manufacture of tanning extracts from bark and wood." In addition to his wife, his father, Bradford; his sister, Nellie; and her husband, George H. Dunston (1851-1912), lived in the house.

George Dunston was a prominent lithographer who derived much of his business from printing can labels. In fact, his firm was among the first to do such work. (Interestingly, Horace Reed, his neighbor at 94, was also a lithographer.) Dunston had to forego college to enter the workforce immediately

102 Oakland Place

This is a grand Shingle style manse, with beautiful proportion and detail. The brick first floor rises from a battered base with stone belt course; it imparts a solid, substantial appearance, yet there is considerable openness in the façade. A massive double entry arch, enhanced by projecting brick details, encompasses both the recessed entry door and the porte cochère. An open arched loggia is located above the deep porch. The preservation of the loggia is unusual; such features were often enclosed in later years to create more interior space. The shingle-clad second floor is illustrative of the subtle detailing typical of the style: rows of saw-tooth shingles line the bottom, while the top features both saw-tooth and tongue-cut shingles. In fact, these bands deflect around the arches of the loggia. The high hip roof with flaring eaves is pierced by tall chimneys and a variety of dormers; the largest has its own prominent gable of saw-tooth shingles with a round-top window beneath a shingled arch.

Circa 1901.   BUFFALO & ERIE COUNTY HISTORICAL SOCIETY

The paneled front door leads into a grand stair hall with a beamed ceiling. With Richardsonian newel posts and Colonial balusters, the wide staircase rises dramatically to the second floor. The original four-paneled window at the landing was made of amber leaded glass; today, the two center panels have clear glass panes. A four-paneled window of green bottle glass is located within a segmental arch below the landing, and a shell arch caps a small doorway beneath the stairs. The large living room is dominated by a grand five-panel bay window with leaded glass transoms, framed by Corinthian pilasters, offering an unparalleled view of Oakland Place. Another principal feature of the living room is the substantial fireplace, which has a heavy entablature festooned with swags and panels and supported by paired Tuscan columns with egg and dart capitals.

This house was built for insurance agent Edward C. Roth (1859-1955) and his wife, Harriet Weller (died 1924). Construction commenced as soon as the property was acquired in 1891. A native Buffalonian, Roth grew up on Swan Street, attended Central High School, and entered the insurance business around 1880. He was evidently very successful in this line of work for he became principal in his own firm, E. C. Roth & Company, and the owner of this substantial Oakland Place home after little more than a decade in the business. As a result of a merger, his firm became the Armstrong-Roth-Cady Company in 1908. Roth eventually served as its board chairman, remaining active in the firm until the age of 95! (His colleague, Frank W. Fiske, lived down the street at 64.) Roth sold the house in 1942 to Ann Porter (1910-1993) and her husband, James (1911-1994), who lived next door at 100. The Porters maintained the exterior appearance and modified the interior, creating two separate rental units: one in front and one in the rear, and the house has been an elegant rental property ever since. The house was transferred to their son, Buffalo attorney Henry M. Porter, in 1994, and was completely restored and remodeled during the years 1994 and 1995 by Henry and Patty Porter.

Above: Detail of Tuscan columns on living room mantel.
Left: View looking down staircase toward panels of leaded amber glass.

103 Oakland Place

This home was designed in 1891 by William H. Boughton and was apparently his first commission after opening his own architectural office. Typical of the Shingle style, the design relies on massing, rather than details, for effect. The large intersecting gambrel roof, which actually extended down into the second story above the porch, is the main feature of the design. The original wood-shingled roof blended with the wood-shingled siding to create a unified, harmonious composition. An integrated polygonal tower projects from the left side of the façade; it is balanced to the right by a wraparound porch with a semicircular projection above the semicircular entry steps. The porch is topped by a delicate balustrade, which also capped the stair-hall bay on the south side. The Colonial Revival style is suggested through the use of swags on the porch and the Palladian window in the gable.

Examples of Modern Architecture (1895)

The paneled entry hall features an unusual coffered ceiling with rounded moldings highlighted with bead and reel detailing. To the right, beneath twin segmental arches supported by fluted Tuscan columns, a small sitting area with a bay window overlooks the porch. A richly paneled staircase, with colonial balusters and square newels edged in bead and reel motif, winds its way up to the second floor beneath a tall arched window that was originally filled with stained glass.

The living room is the highlight of the interior. Dominating this room is an extraordinary fireplace of iron-spotted buff Roman brick, topped by a lintel of cyclopean quarry-faced stone blocks and a finished mantel carved from a single block of stone. Stubby rough-stone colonettes flank the hearth, and fluted Romanesque columns rise above the mantel. Words cannot adequately convey the splendor and originality of this marvelous creation. The adjacent dining room features white-painted paneling and a corner bay with a window seat. The simple Colonial fireplace here seems petite and delicate compared to the imposing one in the living room.

The house was built for Reverend Henry A. Adams, the rector of St. Paul's Episcopal Cathedral on Shelton Square in downtown Buffalo. However, Adams was apparently summoned for a new assignment in another city shortly after moving into his new home. Reverend William S. Hubbell, pastor of the North Presbyterian Church, then moved into the house. After Hubbell left in the late 1890s, the house was evidently rented to a variety of tenants, including William A. Douglas, an attorney who had previously lived across the street at 116.

Above: The living room is dominated by a massive fireplace, the most extraordinary on Oakland Place.

Below: An early view of the living room (library) showing the original beamed ceiling.

Examples of Modern Architecture (1895)

BUFFALO & ERIE COUNTY HISTORICAL SOCIETY

Seymour P. White (1873-1937) and his wife, Annie, moved into the house around 1917. James P. White, Seymour's father, had built the original White Building at 292-298 Main Street. James passed it on to his son and Seymour later replaced it in 1905 with a new building that still stands. As the owner, Seymour managed it until he passed away in 1937; he also served as vice president of the Buffalo Savings Bank.

After White's death, 103 Oakland Place was occupied by William I. Morey. A graduate of Harvard Law, Morey followed a long-standing family tradition by practicing law. His father, Joseph H. Morey, was a prominent attorney and his grandfather, Norris Morey, was responsible for the construction of 107 Oakland Place. His mother, Katrina Van Tassel Williams, was a great-grand niece of author Washington Irving. The house was altered into a two family dwelling in 1950, but the present owners have returned it to a single family home.

Behind 103 sits 101 Oakland Place. One of the oldest homes on the street, this house is much smaller than the street's grand mansions. It was originally part of the Jewett Richmond estate at 844 Delaware Avenue. Historians are not certain whether it was built here or moved to this location for use as servants' quarters around 1880. By 1899, it had acquired the address of 103 Oakland Place. In the early 1930s, it was occupied by caretaker Charles Scott and his wife, Jane. Later, housekeeper Anna Morrison lived here. By the early 1950s, Allan R. Dyte lived in the home with his wife, Helen. Allan Dyte served as the playground director for the city's department of parks. The Dytes added a new open porch and installed a dormer in 1953.

107 Oakland Place

Is there an apartment house in the sacrosanct environment of Oakland Place? Yes, but like everything else on the street, it is of exceptional quality. The building was constructed in 1909 and is one of the few cooperative buildings in Buffalo today. Norris Morey (1838-1920), a prominent attorney, developed the idea after his other apartment house, at 857 Delaware Avenue, was positively received. The Delaware Avenue building still stands, but its original semicircular porch no longer graces the front. It was described thus:

> **A charming little building on Delaware Avenue is the Morey, designed by H. Osgood Holland, who endeavored to disfigure the street as little as possible by giving his design the appearance of a residence as nearly as might be.**
> *Brickbuilder* (Sept. 1902)

Figuring that if such a building was acceptable on the grandest section of Buffalo's illustrious Delaware Avenue, it would be acceptable on Oakland Place. Morey retained Holland to produce another design that would "disfigure the street as little as possible." Morey's interest extended beyond merely construction: when the building was completed, he occupied one of the apartments.

Three stories high and six bays wide, the building is fronted by a colossal portico and capped by a classical cornice and parapet. Holland's attempt to "disfigure the street as little as possible" appears to have been successful: the house blends in well because it looks like a large Colonial Revival single-family residence. The entry door is surrounded by sidelights that curve into a transom; above the door is an iron balcony.

The vestibule, with marble wainscoting and wood pilasters, leads to an open iron staircase with brass railings. Although the apartment house originally had only a service elevator, an additional elevator was installed near the front staircase for residents' use. There are two apartments on each floor, for a total of six units; each is as large as a moderately sized house. Each apartment has a gracious living room with a wood-burning fireplace, two bedrooms, two bathrooms, sitting room, dining room with fireplace, and a kitchen. Although all of the apartments still have their original doors, hardware, and floors of quarter-sawn oak, some changes have been made over the years. Each apartment originally had two small rooms and a bathroom at the rear for servants, but in most cases these have been reconfigured.

Norris Morey was a prominent citizen of the City of Buffalo. He served as a cavalry officer in the Civil War and enjoyed a distinguished legal career, including a partnership with Henry W. Sprague of 65 Oakland Place. His public service included stints as assistant district attorney and assistant city attorney in the early 1870s. In addition, he was nominated as the Republican candidate for mayor in 1882 and selected by President Benjamin Harrison to serve as solicitor general of the United States; he declined both posts for business reasons. He died here at the age of 82, less than a month after retiring from his practice. His grandson, William, later lived next door at 103.

Brickbuilder (Sept. 1902) BUFFALO & ERIE COUNTY PUBLIC LIBRARY

Members of many prominent Buffalo families rented apartments in Morey's Oakland Place building over the years. Tenants included Norris Morey's son, Arthur N. Morey, Loran L. Lewis, Jr., Albert K. Root, Joseph W. Donner, John S. Noyes, and Harry H. Larkin. After World War II the building became a co-op: each unit is purchased by buying a share of the corporation that owns the building.

Above: 857 Delaware Avenue, designed in 1901 by H. Osgood Holland, was the prototype for 107 Oakland Place.

Above left: Each floor plan features a spacious living room with views into Oakland Place (Apartment No. 1).

Left: The elegant dining rooms have fireplaces and low wainscoting (Apartment No. 6).

110 Oakland Place

This address is most notable for what was *not* built here: Frank Lloyd Wright's Darwin D. Martin House. As an executive of the Larkin Soap Company, Darwin Martin had the financial wherewithal to choose from Buffalo's most exclusive neighborhoods. Oakland Place was exactly the sort of street on which Martin and his wife, Isabelle, wished to live. They purchased this lot for their new home as 1901 was drawing to a close. However, their architect, Frank Lloyd Wright, declared that the lot was too small for the sort of house he envisioned. By late 1902, he had convinced them that the most appropriate location for their new home was a large corner site on Jewett Parkway in the Parkside neighborhood.

The Martins did not sell their Oakland Place property even after their new home was completed. In late 1908, Darwin Martin asked Frank Lloyd Wright to prepare plans for an apartment house on the property. Martin's vision was not realized and he sold the lot to James A. White early the following year.

White, president of the Buffalo Maple Flooring Company, immediately retained the prominent architectural firm of Colson & Hudson to design a traditional home. Oak floors were nearly

The breakfast room.

universal at that time and one cannot help but wonder whether he specified his own product for the floors in his new home. His large Colonial Revival house, constructed in 1909, is typical of many Buffalo homes in that its entry façade faces the side rather than the street. This arrangement allowed the living room to span the entire width of the house.

James A. White and his wife, Mary J. Beach, lived at 110 Oakland Place for almost a decade. Edward C. Strong and his wife, Edith Childs, moved in around 1919. Strong was vice president and general manager of the Atlas Steel Casting Company. It appears that Oakland Place was popular with the firm's officers: Clinton R. Wycoff, treasurer and later president, lived at 48, and his son, also an officer at Atlas, at 27. Despite the street's popularity with his colleagues, the Strongs sold their home by 1928.

Elbert S. Bennett and his wife, Lillian Baker, became the new owners of 110 Oakland Place. A native of Pennsylvania, Bennett had worked for the F. W. Woolworth Company since 1898; he moved to Buffalo in 1912 as assistant superintendent when the local S. H. Knox 5-and-10-cent stores were merged into F. W. Woolworth & Company. (The S. H. Knox chain was the initial source of wealth for the Knox family, including Seymour, who lived at 57.) After Elbert retired in 1927, the Bennetts traveled extensively. In 1928, they commissioned architect Frederick C. Backus to transform their newly purchased home on Oakland Place. This transformation left very little of the original interior; it was akin to a new home for Elbert and Lillian.

The outside was changed as well. On the street façade, the original windows were replaced by French doors leading to a new terrace. French doors also replaced the windows on the second story; in this case, the doors lead to iron balconies. The façade also featured a new, rather unusual touch: a new chimney rising through its center. The low hip roof pierced by numerous pedimented dormers is original. The original rough-textured brick facing is intact but it was painted by a previous owner. The garage is still dark red, the original color of the house.

The elegant and substantial entry bay also dates from the remodeling. Inside the at-grade front door, a short staircase leads to a glass door, and then on into the living room. The living room, which extends across the front of the house, has a mantel with Corinthian columns and a swag motif. The swag motif is repeated in the leaded glass doors of the built-in bookcases. The adjacent dining room has a bay window and built-in china cabinets; it leads to a charming breakfast room, where arched windows of leaded glass overlook the back yard.

The second floor is accessed via a Rococo wrought-iron staircase that is located to the right of the entry. As the staircase winds its way to the second floor, the landing features casement windows with colored glass and silhouettes of Apollo and Daphne. Beyond the staircase is a little gem of a library, with paneled walls and a beamed ceiling with the original painted decoration. It is likely that this was Elbert's room: there is a humidor amid the built-in file drawers and the room even had its own built-in exhaust fan. Elbert died in the home in 1943, at the age of 75, and Lillian continued living there into the 1960s.

The staircase is distinguished by richly detailed wrought-iron balustrades.

115 Oakland Place

The houses at 115 and 119 Oakland Place, two of the earliest on the street, were built simultaneously for brothers George and Frank Sickels. Designed in the Queen Anne style, 115 features a great gable on the street façade. This façade also has a band of windows recessed beneath a large shingled arch. A fine veranda originally fronted most of the first floor. In the southwest corner of the house, an unusual rounded bay projected from the living room. Unfortunately, both the veranda and the bay were replaced by a row of French doors when the house was remodeled in the 1920s. The home's north façade features a beautiful leaded glass staircase bay window with an unusual incomplete shingle arch rising above it, adding a touch of whimsy.

The home's interior is similar to the interior of 119: there is a grand staircase hall past the vestibule, a large living room across the front of the home, and a den and dining room behind the living room. The two homes shared a stable behind the properties. Developer Hugh Perry subsequently demolished the stable in 1956 when he was constructing St. George's Square.

This residence was built for George Sickels and his wife Belle in 1891. George was the first realtor to live on Oakland Place. His business touched on all aspects of real estate. An advertisement from that era noted:

> [He conducts] a general real estate business, buying, selling and exchanging all kinds of city and country property on commission, and gives personal attention also to the collection of rents and the management of estates. Investments are desirably placed, likewise, and bonds and mortgages negotiated, while money to any amount is loaned on realty or approved collateral security. *Illustrated Buffalo* (1890)

The Sickels lived at 115 Oakland Place only until 1898. At that time, Clara and W. Eugene Richmond moved into the house. Richmond's father, Dean Richmond of Batavia, was the former president of the New York Central Railroad and the first to import steel rails into America. In 1906, at the age of 58, W. Eugene Richmond died in the house. His wife, Clara, continued to live there with family. During the late 1920s, Charles R. Smith and Maurice M. Wall lived there with their spouses. The Walls had previously rented at 107.

Around 1930, Evan Hollister (1875-1943) and his wife, Ruth Albright (1879-1953), moved in. Hollister, one of many prominent lawyers on the street, once declared, "A trial lawyer's work is never humdrum, for no two cases are alike, and each one affords a glimpse of a different human problem." When he was not working on cases, he spent a great deal of time at home in his well-stocked library. Ruth Albright Hollister was the daughter of John J. Albright, the prominent industrialist. When Ruth was sixteen years old, her mother died. Out of concern for his daughter, Albright asked Smith College to send a young woman to Buffalo to be Ruth's companion. The

Circa 1901.

Detail of staircase.

View looking down staircase to curved landing bay.

young graduate they sent was so companionable that she soon became the second Mrs. Albright! Although it was unusual for women to attend college at that time, Ruth's new mother fully supported her educational goals, and Ruth graduated from Smith College in 1900. Ruth Albright Hollister is known for being one of the founders of the Garret Club. She lived at 115 Oakland Place until her death in 1953. Her brother, Langdon, lived across the street at 120.

Oakland Place

116

This home exemplifies how many of the earliest dwellings on Oakland Place were altered to correspond with new ideas of architectural design in the early twentieth century. Completed in 1893, the house combined a heavy base with a lighter superstructure: the first floor had buff-colored brick and the second floor and roof were done in wood shingles. Tall and narrow, the building had a strong vertical emphasis that was enhanced by the pronounced flaring of the eaves on the high hip roof and the front dormer. The entire composition was suggestive of an arrow pointing upwards. The home was designed as a wedding gift, so it may not be coincidental that the exterior design has diamonds as a theme. Note the raised brickwork that forms a pattern of diamonds along the top of the first story. The pattern is also present, in a vertical form, on the towering chimney. Finally, diamond-cut shingles were arranged to form a diamond pattern in the gable of the front dormer. A faceted entry porch with slender columns and a second-floor balustrade originally graced the front façade. Adjacent to it was a two-story bay, and another bay rose on the south side, culminating in a tower. The present exterior appearance, including vinyl siding on the upper stories and painted brick, is very different from the home's original façade.

As tastes changed after World War I, the front porch was removed and the main entry was relocated to the side bay. This probably coincided with the enlargement of the house in 1928, when a large two-story hip roof addition was placed on the rear. A one-story sunroom topped by a delicate balustrade was also added at that time. The enlargement coincided with extensive interior remodeling. The original front entry vestibule was removed, and the living room was extended across the entire width of the home. The living room's restrained fireplace features simple Colonial moldings and it is flanked by built-in bookshelves. Behind the living room, the entry hall also spans the width of the home. At the north end of the hall is a Colonial staircase with widely spaced balusters. The adjacent rear staircase is one of the few surviving original elements; its detailed newel and closely spaced balusters echo the appearance of the original main staircase. French doors lead from the main hall into the dining room, which has simple low wainscoting and a bay window. The well-lit sunroom is located beyond the dining room. Three steps lead down into the library, the finest room in the house. The simply detailed fireplace is topped by a section of natural wood paneling instead of a mantel, following the style in the late 1920s when mantels were said to encourage clutter. Full-height, built-in bookcases line the walls on either side of the fireplace. The room is graced by a flat plaster ceiling with an alternating pattern of flowers in relief, and a plaster frieze of grapevine motif extends around the room. A bay with French doors leads out onto the stone terrace and into the back yard.

Eric L. Hedstrom had this house designed in 1892 as a wedding present for his daughter. A wholesale dealer and shipper of coal, coke, and pig iron, Hedstrom is known for donating land for the Delaware Avenue Baptist Church. The church was constructed in 1894-1895 and a large mosaic memorial within provides testament to his generosity.

Alice Hedstrom and her husband, William A. Douglas (1859-1921), moved into their new home in 1893. One of many lawyers on Oakland Place, Douglas was concerned with tenement house conditions during the early 1890s, and as an influential private citizen he helped pass ordinances to improve living conditions. He sponsored a bill with architect Williams Lansing (29) and others for the appropriation of a free bathhouse to serve the poor. Douglas also served as president of the Albright Art Gallery from 1913 until 1916. By that time, he had moved across the street to 103, and 116 was occupied by James H. McNulty. McNulty was treasurer and general manager of varnish and paint manufacturer Pratt & Lambert, whose main office and plant were located on Tonawanda Street until a merger in the 1990s. McNulty had the interior of 116 Oakland Place altered in 1914 according to plans by Esenwein & Johnson.

The house was enlarged and further altered in 1928 by the next owners, Harold T. Clement (1890-1971) and his wife, Constance. They lived here after selling their previous home at 29/33 Oakland Place in 1923. Clement was treasurer of the Rogers Brown Iron Co., and later served as executive secretary of the Buffalo Society of Natural Sciences. After World War II, Daniel W. Streeter and his wife, Gertrude, lived in the house. Streeter was president of the Municipal Civil Service Commission.

Above: View in the elegantly appointed library, which was added to the house in the late 1920s.

119 Oakland Place

This large cross-gable Queen Anne style home is one of a pair built for two brothers shortly after Oakland Place was created. This house was constructed for lawyer Frank E. Sickels and his wife, Annie, in 1891. Frank's brother, George, was having his house built next door, at 115 Oakland Place, at the same time.

The houses are similar in massing and plan, but different in many of the details. This home rises from a Medina sandstone foundation and has clapboard siding on the first two stories. In contrast, 115 has shingles on the second story. This home's chimney is brick interspersed with stone for picturesque effect, while the chimney at 115 is solid brick. The massive shingled gable is the most dramatic exterior feature of this home. The beautiful foliate pediment was carved on individual boards that were then

Circa 1901.

set in place in the gable. During the late 1920s the exterior was covered in stucco, and this detail was obscured for many years. Remodeling at that time included removal of the front porch.

The layout is comparable to that of 115 and typical of the period: all of the principal rooms on the first floor can be accessed through the main hall. The present interior reflects both the 1891 design and the remodeling of 1927. The entrance vestibule, with its wainscoting and paneled ceiling, is original. In the main hall, the staircase, which features an iron railing, was altered and a colored glass window was installed at the landing during the remodeling. The living room's arched openings and simple stone fireplace are characteristic of 1920s design, while the adjacent den retains the original beamed ceiling and unusual triple window. With its tall wainscoting and crossbeam ceiling, the dining room is one of the finest spaces in the house. Some of the woodwork throughout the house is now painted white; it would originally have been finished in a natural stain.

Frank and Annie Sickels lived here until 1902, when the house was sold to another lawyer, James E. Ford (1838-1905). A native of Buffalo and a partner in Ford & Ferguson, James specialized in real estate and settling estates. Ford was not able to enjoy his home for very long; he died approximately three years after moving in. His wife, Caroline, lived in the house until her death in 1924. The house passed to her children, who sold it in 1927 to Laura Clark, wife of Dr. Alfred H. Clark, a prominent surgeon. The Clarks immediately remodeled portions of the interior. Working on behalf of Buffalo's poor during the 1930s, Laura Clark was president of the board of the College Creche, a daycare center for working mothers.

Laura's father was hardware merchant Harry Walbridge, who died in 1924, soon after the completion of the new Walbridge Building (Bley & Lyman), at the corner of Court and Franklin Streets. Her mother died in this home in 1932. Interestingly, Laura's uncle Charles lived in 120 across the street long before the Clarks took up residence here, so Laura's connection with Oakland Place was quite long. The Clarks lived in the house until their pasing, he in 1966 and she in 1972.

In 1927 the Clarks removed the porch, covered the house in stucco and made interior modifications in line with the styles of that time. The subsequent owners, Robert and Peggy Moriarty, removed the stucco from the front section of the house and added a new front porch in 2002, restoring the original appearance to a great extent.

[Photos of this home, interior and exterior, were taken during the ownership of Robert and Peggy Moriarty (1972-2006).]

Above: Unusual round-top door in dining room.
Opposite: The elegantly appointed dining room is a most charming space.

120 Oakland Place

Although this is one of the most substantial and imposing homes on the street, the narrow lot disguises its size. The house is not easily slotted into a stylistic category, but the exterior has the simple, solid quality often associated with the later works of H. H. Richardson. Designed in 1895, it was one of the earliest commissions for local architect Martin C. Miller. Here he created a massive dwelling of Roman brick, rendered in a rich color pallet ranging from yellow to brown. The roof is composed of two massive side gable sections linked by a hyphen. The arched front entryway is flanked by a projecting polygonal porch with Tuscan columns on the right and a massive round bay on the left. Both are now missing the balustrades of Gothic tracery that

Present owner: Dr. Constantine and Nitsa Karakousis

originally added so much to the exterior composition. Piercing the roof are twin dormers with tiny blank oval openings in the pediment, which echo the small oval window of leaded glass above the entry.

The home's entryway, which has a fine mosaic floor, leads to one of the most spectacular spaces on Oakland Place: an enormous polygon-shaped main hall. Ionic pilasters in four corners support a wide cross-beamed ceiling. A large, open sitting room lies to the left and a grand staircase to the right. Under a stained glass skylight, the flight of stairs rises past leaded glass windows, the newel posts echoing the rich classical details found throughout the first floor. The main hall also features a fireplace surrounded by unique rough-faced brick, topped by a mantel supported by Ionic columns that are crowned by capitals with unusually thin profiles. An original bathroom is located beneath the staircase. In the front of the house are a small library and a large living room, where a coved ceiling encompasses the rounded bay of the

Circa 1901 view of house shows the original Gothic balustrades that are now gone. BUFFALO & ERIE COUNTY HISTORICAL SOCIETY

tower. Both library and living room have arched marble fireplaces that likely came from the original owner's previous mid-nineteenth century home. Beyond the main hall, a small sitting room leads to the dining room, which has natural woodwork, a coved ceiling, and French doors leading to the rear terrace. As one of the largest homes on Oakland Place, it is worth noting that upon opening the front door, a guest is afforded a view extending all the way to the rear of the house.

This grand dwelling was commissioned in 1895 by Anna F. Walbridge. She spent the rest of her life here with her husband, Buffalo native Charles E. Walbridge (1841-1913), and their children. Charles had served throughout the Civil War as a quartermaster, handling the massive logistical needs of various Union armies, and rose to the rank of lieutenant colonel. After the war, he returned to Buffalo and in 1884 founded Walbridge & Company, reputedly the largest hardware business in the state outside New York City. (His niece Laura Clark

later lived across the street at 119.) Anna died in 1910 and Charles passed away in 1913. After his death, his daughters lived in the house. Insurance agent Richard L. Wood later occupied the residence.

During the 1920s, Langdon Albright (1880-1962) moved into the house with his family and lived here until his death. The second son of industrialist John J. Albright, Langdon had previously lived at 33. In 1914, he moved into a large new house adjacent to his father's mansion on West Ferry Street. (Both of those mansions are now gone.) The senior Albright's reversal of fortune during the early 1920s evidently affected Langdon as well: he left his West Ferry Street home and returned to Oakland Place. His sister, Ruth Albright Hollister, lived across the street at 115.

Langdon, who was trained as an electrical engineer, served as vice president of the Niagara, Lockport & Ontario Power Company. He also served as a longtime trustee of the Albright Art Gallery. Like architect Edward B. Green, he was opposed to the gallery's acquisition of avant garde art, spearheaded by A. Conger Goodyear, who lived around the corner at 160 Bryant Street. Albright, Green, and other conservative gallery members were especially scandalized by the acquisition of Picasso's *La Toilette* in 1926, and they ensured that Goodyear was not reelected to the board three years later. By then, Goodyear had moved to New York City where he soon became the first president of the Museum of Modern Art. Prior to leaving Buffalo, though, he kindled an interest in modern art in Seymour Knox (57). For Knox, this interest grew into a lifelong passion. One wonders what Albright might have thought about Knox's modernist transformation of the Albright Art Gallery, both inside and out, in the years after World War II. After Langdon Albright's death in 1962, engineer Thomas H. Danforth moved into 120.

Above: The rounded bay of the living room is a dramatic feature.

Left: Main hall looking towards front door, with library and living room on either side.

Far Left: View from front door through the spectacular main hall and into the dining room beyond.

Opposite: Three views of the grand main staircase, showing the richly detailed newels and balusters and the magnificent stained glass skylight above.

123 Oakland Place

The house that currently stands at 123 Oakland Place is another example of a dwelling with wanderlust: it originally stood at 178 Bryant Street.

This Queen Anne style dwelling has a richly varied exterior rising above a limestone foundation, with clapboards on the first story and shingles above. The front façade features a bay beneath an expansive gable supported by large shingled brackets. The gable contains a window band with a geometric transom sash and an arrow-slit opening at the peak. The north elevation has two bays, one faceted and one rounded; the latter is topped with a foliate band. The house has retained much of its original appearance, both inside and out. A new porch that closely approximates the long-lost original was completed in 2005.

The entry leads to a large, richly paneled entry hall, which is dominated by a grand staircase that cascades into the center of the room from an open hallway on the second floor. The balustrade is an unusual combination of spindles and arches, and the newel posts have chamfered corners with bead-and-reel decoration. Pocket doors lead to the living and dining rooms, and all of the door and window casings feature fluted pilasters topped by squared sunburst motifs. This incredible space also features a richly molded cornice and built-in seats beneath leaded glass windows. The most interesting feature of the generously proportioned living room is the rounded bay window with a beautifully detailed radiator that matches the curve of the bay. The dining room, sheathed in the same wainscoting as the hall, features a beamed ceiling and a bay window with leaded glass transoms.

This grand home was built in 1892 for Edwin G. Hoag, an employee of prominent realtor L. F. W. Arend. Ella Goodyear subsequently purchased the property around 1911. The widow of lumber baron Charles W. Goodyear, Ella, who lived at 888 Delaware Avenue, wanted each of her three children to have homes opening onto her large back yard. She also wanted the property at 178 Bryant Street as the site of a new home for her daughter, Esther, and Esther's husband, Arnold Watson. In late 1911 or early 1912, the house was lifted up, pushed back, turned ninety degrees, and placed in its present location at 123 Oakland Place. The entire process took place on the grounds of the extensive Goodyear property.

Per Ella's wishes, the house now located at 123 Oakland Place became a home for her second son, Charles W. Goodyear, Jr. (1883-1967), and his wife, Grace Rumsey. After graduating from Yale and marrying Grace, Charles Jr. managed the Goodyear lumber interests in Louisiana, but in 1910 Grace insisted on returning home to Buffalo. In 1914, Ella transferred the house to Grace. Ten years later, as she and her husband prepared to move into their new house at 190 Bryant Street (designed by Bley & Lyman), Grace returned the house to her mother-in-law. Ella then rented out 123.

A unique balustrade highlights the impressive staircase.

The dining room features wainscoting and a beamed ceiling.

Unfortunately for Charles and Grace, their new home was not a happy one. Charles had "strayed off the marital reservation," and was having an affair with S. V. R. Spaulding's wife, Marion. The affair scandalized Buffalo society, and the pair became *personae non gratae* in many quarters. Charles was even forbidden entry into the home of his brother-in-law, Arnold Watson, next door at 180 Bryant Street. Eventually Charles and Marion divorced their spouses and in 1935 married each other. Ella transferred 123 Oakland Place in 1936 to her daughter, Esther Watson. Esther's daughter, Ellen, subsequently moved into this house with her new husband, S. V. R. Spaulding, Jr.—an ironic twist, inasmuch as Spaulding Jr. was the son of Charles Goodyear's new wife.

In 1953, B. Mason Bowen, a realtor with Gurney, Overturf & Becker, and his wife, Jean, moved into the house from the former carriage house at 80, where they had been living. They made 123 Oakland Place their home until 1972.

123 Oakland Place at its original location of 178 Bryant Street.

Oakland Place

126

This magnificent manor house, built by one of Buffalo's most prominent master builders, is actually the second home on this site. The original was a frame Colonial Revival dwelling that was evidently constructed in 1894-1895, when the property was considerably narrower than it is now. This house had a prominent front bay with a full-width front porch, shingled gables with Palladian windows, and a porte cochère along the north side. It appears to have been constructed by Eli D. Hofeller, a builder and real estate dealer, as a speculative home. After a frequently changing array of occupants, John and Josephine Cowper took up residence in 1917 and remained at this address for the rest of their lives. The Cowpers were fairly new to the city, but they were somewhat familiar with Oakland Place because they had previously rented across the street at 143.

124 Oakland Place, circa 1901. Demolished 1928.

John W. Cowper (1871-1944) was a native of Virginia, where his father had served in the Confederate army. Cowper initially worked as a civil engineer on railroad projects before entering the contracting business with John Stewart & Company of New York. He supervised the construction of many of the firm's projects in America and England, including the Savoy Hotel in London. After working for other firms, he moved to Buffalo in 1914 and founded the Cowper Construction Company the following year. Cowper's firm was an instant success, managing numerous projects throughout the nation. His firm's Buffalo projects included City Hall, the Rand Building, the Buffalo Athletic Club, and the Courier-Express Building, as well as many others.

Cowper decided that his success merited a new home, and in 1928 he commissioned Hudson & Hudson to create the design. He had aquired additional land for this construction project. In 1919 his lot size had expanded considerably when he purchased land that had previously been part of the backyard of 226 Bryant Street (which is now 138 Oakland Place). This same division of land allowed for the construction of 130 Oakland Place in 1921. Hudson & Hudson

Detail of Carrera glass in upstairs bathroom.

designed a grand Tudor Revival manse with an exterior of stucco trimmed in stone and bands of stone-framed casement windows. The side gable design is braced by massive stone end chimneys, and the roof slates get smaller and thinner as they rise, a common feature in homes of this style. The off-center projecting entry bay introduces a note of asymmetry to the formal composition; a stone in the gable gives the date of construction.

The stone entry arch leads to the main hall containing a curved staircase and wrought-iron balusters rising beneath a chandelier. A library to the left of the entrance features full-height paneling and a concave plaster ceiling with a relief of small birds in flight. The living room behind the library was built to accommodate centuries-old wood paneling taken from Monmouth House in Wales. The large medieval fireplace is a carved stone replica of the original, and the plaster ceiling border features an alternating owl, dog, rabbit, and rooster pattern. The dining room, located across the entry hall, has china closets hidden behind doors in the paneling and leaded glass doors that lead out to the stone terrace. Upstairs, the rooms have Art Deco detailing, the most notable of which is in the original bathroom, where the walls are covered in black, white, gold, and blue Carrera glass, topped with a frieze of mythological creatures.

In 1929, just as Cowper began building Buffalo's City Hall, the family moved into their new home. Cowper died in the house in 1944, at the age of 73, following four years of poor health. The Cowpers' only child, John Jr., died a year later of pneumonia at the age of 36, and his funeral was held at the family home. Josephine lived in the house until her death in 1968.

Above: Curving main staircase with wrought-iron balusters.

Left: Master bathroom features walls of multicolored Carrera glass with Art Deco detailing. The original bathroom fixtures remain intact.

Above: Centuries-old paneling taken from a British manor house is the outstanding feature of the spacious living room.

Above right: Intricate classical details highlight the dining room ceiling.

Right: Original light fixtures still adorn the walls.

129 Oakland Place

This fine home was designed in 1907 by Lansing & Beierl for one of the city's most distinguished lawyers. It shares an architectural identity crisis with 28. The exterior is a fine rendition of the Craftsman style, with exposed rafter tails beneath the hipped roof, prominent brackets, and shingle sheathing. The façade was originally a balanced composition, with the generous entrance porch offset by a wide bay window. In 1911, a library wing, which repeated the large bay window of the original house, was added to the north side by Lansing, Bley & Lyman. This addition gives the home its present asymmetrical appearance.

In contrast to the exterior, the interior is Colonial Revival. The vestibule, which features built-in coat closets, leads to the large wainscoted main hall that is dominated by a Colonial staircase rising to the second floor. A large arched stained glass window on the landing is one of the most impressive on the street. The woodwork, originally stained, is now painted white. Wide openings in the main hall lead to the principal rooms, resulting in the first floor being essentially one large space (see page 12). All of the door and window casings have ears, which were apparently popular with Lansing & Beierl, as indicated by their presence in other houses they designed on Oakland Place. The expansive living room features a wide fireplace with paired Ionic columns and a bay window with a large original picture window and leaded glass transoms. The adjacent dining room likewise has a wide fireplace, and walls covered by fabric panels. On the opposite side of the hall, pocket doors open onto a stairway that leads down into the 1911 library addition. This room has a yellow brick fireplace, built-in bookshelves, and a beamed ceiling. A trap door next to the fireplace leads into the basement.

The house was built for Lyman M. Bass (1876-1955), who had a reputation as one of Buffalo's most vigorous and aggressive trial lawyers. His father, Lyman K., had practiced law with Grover Cleveland. His mother, Frances Metcalfe, who had a strong literary bent, was regarded as one of the city's most brilliant socialites. After studying at Yale, where he played end on the varsity football team, Lyman M. fought in the Spanish-American War. In 1900 he received his law degree from Harvard. Not long after returning to Buffalo, he became a partner in one of the city's oldest firms, Kenefick, Cooke, Mitchell & Bass, remaining with the firm until his death. His obituary noted his work ethic: "Behind his moves and arguments lay long hours of patient and painstaking preparation and attention to detail." As a colleague reported, "Those who worked with him on some major trials felt the only reason he slept at all was because he eventually found himself alone with no one left to help him. His assistants would become so exhausted that one by one they'd drag themselves off to rest, although Mr. Bass was all for 'keeping at it.'" ("Lyman M. Bass, Noted Lawyer for Half Century, Dies," *Buffalo News*, July 9, 1955; source for both quotes.)

His reputation was such that in 1906 President Theodore Roosevelt appointed him U.S. attorney for Western New York. Bass was also an avid hunter: "The mounted heads of some of his targets adorned his law-office wall, staring down glassy-eyed upon numerous gold and silver marksmanship trophies." (Ibid.) Some of those heads still adorn the walls of the library at 129. Lyman married Grace Holland in 1904, and their three daughters were later regarded as among the loveliest and most eligible ladies in the city. Grace Bass, one of the founders of the Garret club, lived in the house until her death in 1960. Frank E. Wattles, an egg and cheese merchant at the Niagara Frontier Food Terminal, subsequently purchased the house. Wattles had previously lived at 48.

An impressive Colonial Revival staircase leads up to the second floor beneath an exquisite arched window of clear glass highlighted by stained glass details.

PRESENT OWNERS: MR. AND MRS. WILLIAM J. WILLIAMSON, JR.

130 Oakland Place

This beautiful home has a touch of irony about it: built on what was once a backyard, it has no backyard of its own! The land on which it sits was formerly part of the deep, narrow lot of 226 Bryant Street (now 138), which extended 190 feet down Oakland Place, into what is now 126. The land was subdivided into smaller parcels in 1919. One piece served to expand the lot next door at 126. Anna L. Burnett, widow of Charles H. Burnett, purchased the lot at 130 for the house she had built for herself in 1921. Mrs. Burnett selected a Colonial Revival design, with a symmetrical three-bay façade and a small entry porch. Interesting touches include an exterior of shingles instead of clapboards, front windows with their own sidelights, and a gambrel roof with an almost imperceptible change of pitch.

Upon stepping past the solid panel front door framed by sidelights and a fanlight, one enters a stair hall that bisects the dwelling from front to back. The staircase, with its Tuscan newel and slender tapered balusters, rises straight up to the open second floor hall with no turns. The tasteful living room, which features built-in bookshelves, is located to the left of the entrance. A morning room lies beyond the living room, and the dining room is located to the right of the hall. The simply detailed rooms have tall, plain baseboards and Adamesque door hardware. The heavy marble-arched fireplaces in the living room and main bedroom are likely from a much earlier residence. They may have come from the original owner's former home; they were likely removed and installed in this home for sentimental reasons, a not unusual practice at the time. The second-floor rooms have their original built-in closets. Interestingly, two of the bedroom closets are connected by a secret door.

In 1945, Anna Burnett sold the house to Dorothy Wycoff. Dorothy and her husband, Clinton, lived in the house for only a short time. When they moved to 27 the following year, they sold 130 to Ward A. Wickwire, Jr., and his wife, Jean. The Wickwires did not reside in the house for long, either. They moved to Pittsburgh, selling the house, in 1948, to Nelson and May Graves. Nelson Graves was president of the Barcalo Manufacturing Company, which produced the Barcolounger, the pioneer recliner. The company moved to North Carolina in 1965. The Graves lived in the house until 1974, when it was purchased by William J. Williamson, Jr., a banker, and his wife, Nanette Swift. Nanette died in 1978. In 1980, Mr. Williamson married Evelyn B. Ewart, a widow.

Vignettes of 130: Living room, arched marble fireplace, and original light fixture.

PRESENT OWNER: PETER J. WOLFE

135 Oakland Place

As is the case with two other houses on Oakland Place, the circa 1887 house at 135 was previously located elsewhere: at 239 Bryant Street. This house, however, has the distinction of being the only one to actually move to Oakland Place with its owners. This moderately sized Queen Anne dwelling may seem small when compared with some of the other homes on Oakland Place, but it is typical of many of the middle-class homes that were erected across the city during the late 1880s. A modernized porch extends across the front, a large bay dominates the south elevation, and the house is capped by a picturesque hip roof with projecting gables. The front gable above the second floor contains the most interesting features: a multipane oriel window topped by a carved lion's head within a shingled arch. The exterior surfaces were otherwise greatly simplified when the siding was redone. Originally, the house was probably sided with a mixture of clapboard and shingles with subtle details, similar to 123.

The interior of 135 Oakland Place has been modernized over the years, but recent renovations have restored much of the home's original elegance. In the entry hall, the original spindle staircase winds its way up to the second floor. Many of the other interior details, such as the fluted door casings throughout the first floor, were added later. The living room, to the right of the entry hall, was originally two rooms. Now, it is a large and gracious space with a bay window. A new cornice and wainscot embellish the dining room. The interesting wood-paneled den was a 1950s remodeling of the original kitchen.

The first occupant of the new house at its Bryant Street location was Lucius E. Bartlett (1860-1945). A graduate of Central High School, he studied art in this country and in Europe. When he moved into the house, Bartlett was working for George H. Dunston, the lithographer who later lived at 100. Bartlett subsequently worked as cartoonist for the Buffalo Courier and at the Niagara Lithograph Company, and continued to work as an artist even while he held other positions. A member (and dean) of the Saturn Club, Bartlett greatly contributed to the appearance of the present club building: "He designed the mottoes on the interior walls of the clubrooms, 977 Delaware Ave., the stone cutting of the planet Saturn over the doorway, and other tile, stone and stained glass" (*Courier Express*, Jan. 27, 1945). Bartlett also designed the seal of the University of Buffalo. Moritz Cohn and his family occupied the home after Bartlett.

The last occupants at the Bryant Street location, William and Mary Smith, moved into the house before 1910. In 1911, the property, but not the house, was sold for the site of the new Children's Hospital nurses' home. The nurses' home, which was designed by Lansing, Bley & Lyman, is still standing. As a result of the sale of the property, Mary Smith purchased the lot at 135 Oakland Place from the Union Trust Company of Detroit, and the company obligingly moved the Smith home to the new site. This was significant, for it is not often that people move to a new location without changing houses! William Warren Smith (1872-1951) was added to the deed two years later. A Buffalo native and Yale graduate, William was president of the A. B. Smith Chemical Company at the time of the move. He later became president of the Abstract Title & Mortgage Corporation. In addition, he served as treasurer of Buffalo State College, as president of the Buffalo Fine Arts Academy, and twice as dean of the Saturn Club. Mary Newhall Smith (1873-1951) had been both president and treasurer of Children's Hospital and president of the Garret Club. After the Smiths died in 1951, Dean M. Rockwell, an engineer, and his wife, Virginia, purchased the house. The Rockwells lived at 135 Oakland Place until 2000.

The spindle staircase is one of the few original features remaining in the house.

138 Oakland Place

This is the oldest house on Oakland Place, though it bears little resemblance to its original appearance. It was built circa 1874 for the McAllister family, on a lot purchased by Sarah McAllister in 1873. Oakland Place did not exist at the time of this transaction, so the original address was 226 Bryant Street. The house was narrow and deep, as the lot demanded, and had a strong vertical emphasis. Its original appearance was similar to the homes at 228 and 230 Bryant Street, both of which were built around the same time as this house, now known as 138 Oakland Place.

In 1891, McAllister sold the house to real estate dealer Frederick L. Danforth. It seems that Danforth remodeled the house in the Queen Anne style at the time of the purchase, adding a wide wrap-around porch and making other modifications. Other than the small multipane triple window in the attic of the Bryant Street elevation, no other trace of that remodeling is now evident. After Frederick's death in 1897, the house remained in his family, who rented it to a variety of tenants, including Charles S. Spaulding.

Around 1904, Mrs. Caroline Richards and her family moved into the house. Caroline's husband, Dr. John C. Richards, had died twelve years earlier. In 1919, Caroline's son, John B. Richards (1874-1946), purchased 226 Bryant for her continued use. John was a prominent local lawyer, and he and his sister both lived in the house at various times. The Richards family completely remodeled the house circa 1928, and changed the address to 138 Oakland Place. The house has retained its remodeled appearance. The remodeling included adding a significant amount of space and a new symmetrical Oakland Place façade, featuring two projecting front-gabled wings flanking a recessed entrance beneath a porch.

The interior, with its seven fireplaces, was arranged as a double, or possibly a triple, and was occupied by Mrs. Richards; her son, John; her daughter, Helen; and Helen's husband, Rev. Frederick L. Greene. The second-floor sitting room was accessible from both sides of the house, indicating that some rooms were jointly occupied.

An uncommon treatment today: The dining room features elegant wallpaper, the traditional method of wall covering.

A grand entry hall leads to the dining room and the living room is to the right of the entry hall. The simple décor was in keeping with the austere elegance of the period. Leading to the second floor is a curving staircase with an iron baluster. Behind the staircase is perhaps the most interesting room in the house: a library with full-height vertical board paneling. The room is notable for two secret doors: one that leads to a small washroom and another concealing the original refrigerator.

After John B. Richards died in the house in 1946, ownership passed to his sister, Helen, who sold it in 1947 to William and Edwina Gurney. William Gurney was a realtor in the prominent firm of Gurney, Overturf & Becker (now Gurney, Becker & Bourne), and the uncle of noted playwright A. R. Gurney. The Gurneys lived in the house until 1981.

138 Oakland Place in its previous incarnation as 226 Bryant Street, circa 1901.

138

143 Oakland Place

The double house at 143 Oakland Place is the best example of the Craftsman style on the entire street. It was constructed in 1914 on land that had, until a few years earlier, been a cow pasture. Children attending the Elmwood School across Bryant Street were allowed to play on the vacant lot, provided they left the tethered cow alone! Designed by notable local architect Stephen R. Berry, the house was built by the Elbryoak (Elmwood, Bryant, Oakland) Realty Company as a speculative dwelling. Although the entrance faces the Bryant Street side, the house received an address on the more prestigious Oakland Place.

The design is certainly an anomaly on this elite street. Most wealthy Buffalonians of the day sought the historical allusions associated with designs based on European or American colonial precedents. While these values appealed to many people in the middle class, there were also people who appreciated homes largely free of past architectural elements. For them, the answer was the simply detailed, informal dwellings of the Craftsman era.

This basic, side-gable, two-story home is almost entirely sheathed in unpainted wood shingles. Numerous oriels, projecting from the façades, add variety to the surfaces. The most notable is the large glazed sun porch on the first floor with an inviting open porch above it. The exposed rafter tails beneath the roof of hexagonal slate, simple brackets, and bands of windows are hallmarks of the Craftsman style. In addition, it was designed as a duplex on a street of nearly all single-family homes.

The entry, on the north side of the home, contains the staircase leading to the upper unit. Each unit has a central hall: the living room and dining room are to the west (facing the street), while the bedrooms, bathrooms, and kitchen are along the east side of the house. The living room and dining room in each unit have inlaid hardwood floors. The dining rooms are the most elaborately finished of the spaces, with beamed ceilings and low wainscoting. The open Craftsman staircase in the lower unit leads down to a finished basement that boasts hardwood floors and a large full-height brick fireplace topped by a brick corbelled mantel. The upper unit also enjoys additional space off its main floor; in this case, fine attic space.

The first resident owner was Cora B. Lee, widow of Walter C. Lee. She lived in one unit and rented out the other to a succession of tenants. (It is not known whether she occupied the upper or the lower unit.) Evidently her first tenants were John W. Cowper and his wife, Jean. Cowper had just moved to Buffalo and founded the Cowper Construction Company. The Cowpers liked Oakland Place so much that they soon purchased 126 as their own home. They lived in the existing house for a decade before replacing it with a grander mansion. Mrs. Lee lived at 143 until after World War II. William H. Gurney, Jr., subsequently purchased it. The neighbors included his parents across the street at 138.

Detail of the western bay.

The tastefully appointed living room.